Praise for *Philippians: Verse by Verse*

"Grant Osborne is one of the premier New Testament commentators of our day. This commentary and the series of which it is a part draws upon Dr. Osborne's vast academic and ministry experience, and places it at the disposal of innumerable pastors and teachers around the world. The commentary introduces and treats difficult and critical problems, but the focus is on careful in-depth exposition of the meaning of the text verse by verse and its application in the life of the believer and the church. It is an offering of love to the Lord Jesus and his people that will bear much fruit for generations to come."

—**Richard E. Averbeck**, professor of Old Testament and Semitic languages, director of the PhD program in theological studies, Trinity Evangelical Divinity School

"Grant Osborne embodies the mind of Christ (Phil 2:5–11) as he places his years of expert study in the service of this Pauline message and of the church to which this letter was sent. Students, teachers, mentors, small group leaders, and others will find here a sure-footed and reliable guide to Philippians."

—**Jon C. Laansma**, associate professor of Greek and New Testament, Wheaton College and Graduate School

"Dr. Osborne's latest work on Philippians adds to a commentary series that will become a favorite resource for the many preachers and teachers who are looking for straightforward clarity in both interpreting and applying God's Word. There are rich exegetical insights on every page—including wonderful word studies from the original Greek text—all presented without becoming overly technical or academic. Bible students and communicators will equally appreciate the wealth of practical theology and useable application points which effectively point to the enduring relevance of the message of Philippians."

—**Todd Habegger**, senior pastor, Village Church of Gurnee (IL)

"As with all Grant Osborne's previous writings, this Philippians commentary is excellent. It fills a critical need in the church, bridging the gap between the more technical commentaries available and the needs of the people of God engaged in the world. The exegetical analysis is critically insightful. It fulfills its stated purpose: to provide a resource that will enhance devotional reading of Scripture and biblical studies in local churches. This is appropriate to Philippians and the other writings of the New Testament, as they were written from a deep desire to enhance the spiritual lives of the communities of God's people. I believe that the Apostle Paul would be delighted that this work is available to God's people today."

—**Mark Keown**, senior lecturer in New Testament, Laidlaw College (Auckland, New Zealand)

T0335224

"For years I have found Grant Osborne's commentaries to be reliable and thoughtful guides for those wanting to better understand the New Testament. Indeed, Osborne has mastered the art of writing sound, helpful, and readable commentaries and I am confident that this new series will continue the level of excellence that we have come to expect from him. How exciting to think that pastors, students, and laity will all be able to benefit for years to come from the wise and insightful interpretation provided by Professor Osborne in this new series. The Osborne New Testament Commentaries will be a great gift for the people of God."

—**David S. Dockery**, president, Trinity International University

"One of my most valued role models, Grant Osborne is a first-tier biblical scholar who brings to the text of Scripture a rich depth of insight that is both accessible and devotional. Grant loves Christ, loves the Word, and loves the church, and those loves are embodied in this wonderful new commentary series, which I cannot recommend highly enough."

—**George H. Guthrie**, Benjamin W. Perry Professor of Bible, Union University

"Grant Osborne is ideally suited to write a series of concise commentaries on the New Testament. His exegetical and hermeneutical skills are well known, and anyone who has had the privilege of being in his classes also knows his pastoral heart and wisdom."

—**Ray Van Neste**, professor of biblical studies, director of the
R.C. Ryan Center for Biblical Studies, Union University

"Grant Osborne is an eminent New Testament scholar and warm-hearted professor who loves the Word of God. Through decades of effective teaching at Trinity Evangelical Divinity School and church ministry around the world, he has demonstrated an ability to guide his readers in a careful understanding of the Bible. The volumes in this accessible commentary series help readers understand the text clearly and accurately. But they also draw us to consider the implications of the text, providing key insights on faithful application and preaching that reflect a lifetime of ministry experience. This unique combination of scholarship and practical experience makes this series an invaluable resource for all students of God's Word, and especially those who are called to preach and teach."

—**H. Wayne Johnson**, associate academic dean and associate professor of
pastoral theology, Trinity Evangelical Divinity School

PHILIPPIANS

Verse by Verse

PHILIPPIANS

Verse by Verse

GRANT R. OSBORNE

LEXHAM PRESS

Philippians: Verse by Verse
Osborne New Testament Commentaries

Copyright 2017 Grant R. Osborne

Lexham Press, 1313 Commercial St., Bellingham, WA 98225
LexhamPress.com

Print ISBN 9781683590125
Digital ISBN 9781683590132

Lexham Editorial Team: David Bomar, Elliot Ritzema, Joel Wilcox
Cover Design: Christine Christopherson
Typesetting: ProjectLuz.com

CONTENTS

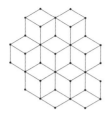

SERIES PREFACE

There are two authors of every biblical book: the human author who penned the words, and the divine Author who revealed and inspired every word. While God did not dictate the words to the biblical writers, he did guide their minds so that they wrote their own words under the influence of the Holy Spirit. If Christians really believed what they said when they called the Bible "the word of God," a lot more would be engaged in serious Bible study. As divine revelation, the Bible deserves, indeed demands, to be studied deeply.

This means that when we study the Bible, we should not be satisfied with a cursory reading in which we insert our own meanings into the text. Instead, we must always ask what God intended to say in every passage. But Bible study should not be a tedious duty we have to perform. It is a sacred privilege and a joy. The deep meaning of any text is a buried treasure; all the riches are waiting under the surface. If we learned there was gold deep under our backyard, nothing would stop us from getting the tools we needed to dig it out. Similarly, in serious Bible study all the treasures and riches of God are waiting to be dug up for our benefit.

This series of commentaries on the New Testament is intended to supply these tools and help the Christian understand more deeply the God-intended meaning of the Bible. Each volume walks the reader verse-by-verse through a book with the goal of opening up for us what God led Matthew or Paul or John to say to their readers. My goal in this series is to make sense of the historical and literary background of these ancient works, to supply the information that will enable the modern reader to understand exactly what the biblical writers were saying to their first-century audience. I want to remove the complexity of most modern commentaries and provide an easy-to-read explanation of the text.

But it is not enough to know what the books of the New Testament meant back then; we need help in determining how each text applies to our lives today. It is one thing to see what Paul was saying his readers in Rome or Philippi, and quite another thing to see the significance of his words for us. So at key points in the commentary, I will attempt to help the reader discover areas in our modern lives that the text is addressing.

I envision three main uses for this series:

1. **Devotional Scripture reading.** Many Christians read rapidly through the Bible for devotions in a one-year program. That is extremely helpful to gain a broad overview of the Bible's story. But I strongly encourage another kind of devotional reading—namely, to study deeply a single segment of the biblical text and try to understand it. These commentaries are designed to enable that. The commentary is based on the NIV and explains the meaning of the verses, enabling the modern reader to read a few pages at a time and pray over the message.

2. **Church Bible studies.** I have written these commentaries also to serve as guides for group Bible studies. Many Bible studies today consist of people coming together and sharing what they think the text is saying. There are strengths in such an approach, but also weaknesses. The problem is that God inspired these scriptural passages so that the

church would understand and obey *what he intended the text to say*. Without some guidance into the meaning of the text, we are prone to commit heresy. At the very least, the leaders of the Bible study need to have a commentary so they can guide the discussion in the direction God intended. In my own church Bible studies, I have often had the class read a simple exposition of the text so they can all discuss the God-given message, and that is what I hope to provide here.

3. **Sermon aids.** These commentaries are also intended to help pastors faithfully exposit the text in a sermon. Busy pastors often have too little time to study complex thousand-page commentaries on biblical passages. As a result, it is easy to spend little time in Bible study and thereby to have a shallow sermon on Sunday. As I write this series, I am drawing on my own experience as a pastor and interim pastor, asking myself what I would want to include in a sermon.

Overall, my goal in these commentaries is simple: I would like them to be interesting and exciting adventures into New Testament texts. My hope is that readers will discover the riches of God that lay behind every passage in his divine word. I hope every reader will fall in love with God's word as I have and begin a similar lifelong fascination with these eternal truths!

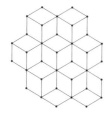

INTRODUCTION TO PHILIPPIANS

GENRE

It is obvious that this is a letter, but there are different kinds of New Testament letters. For instance, Hebrews is more of a treatise, dealing with the superiority of Christ over every aspect of the Jewish religious system, and Ephesians is a homily or word of exhortation dealing with Christ and the church. What kind of letter is Philippians?

1. Letter of friendship—There is a growing recognition that Philippians is primarily a letter of friendship. Courses in letter writing were taught in the ancient world, since that ability was important in both commerce and politics. In one such textbook the friendship letter was the first of twenty-one types discussed. Paul's letter to the Philippians contains several formal signs of being a friendship letter: language expressing affection, such as "I long for all of you with the affection of Christ" (1:8) or "I love and long for" and "my joy and crown" (4:1); unity language, such as that expressing like-mindedness (2:2; 4:2) or oneness (1:27; 2:2; 4:3); fellowship/partnership language (1:5, 7; 3:10; 4:15); language of sharing and caring (1:30; 2:17–18; 4:10, 14–18); expression of the desire to see each other (1:25–26, 27; 2:23, 24); and sharing and asking for personal news (1:12–26). Paul and

Philippi have a deep and abiding friendship. In Philippians 4:15 Paul says that Philippi was the only church to continue supporting him through his ministry, and he felt an abiding joy and a deep sense of gratitude for the believers there.

2. Word of exhortation—Of course, Philippians is more than just a friendship letter. It also is a word of exhortation, as Paul addresses significant needs in the Philippian church; these believers need assistance in handling persecution (1:27–30), reconciling conflict and dissension (2:1–18; 4:2–3), and dealing with false teachers (3:1–4, 18–19). In dealing with such spiritual and moral needs, Philippians more than any other letter uses individuals as paradigms or models of exemplary conduct; these include Jesus (2:5–11), Timothy (2:19–24), Epaphroditus (2:25–30), and Paul himself (3:4–14, 17). The primary quality modeled is humility, as defined in 2:3–4: "Value others above yourselves, not looking to your own interests but each of you to the interests of the others." The path to this is provided in 3:12–14: "Forgetting what is behind and straining toward what is ahead, I press on ... ."

3. Multiple letters—Quite a few commentators believe that Philippians is not a single letter but a compilation of two or three different letters. As we will see in the commentary, 3:1 ("Finally") seemingly introduces an intended conclusion, but it is interrupted with the news of the coming of the **Judaizers**.[1] So Philippians 3:1–4:1 may be seen as an interpolation of a separate letter. Also, many interpreters see 4:10–20 as a distinct letter, given that Paul seems to wait a long time to pen his thanksgiving in these verses for the Philippians' gift to him. A possible explanation is that Paul had already sent an expression of gratitude soon after he received the gift, and a later editor included those

---

1. Terms in bold type are discussed in the glossary (page 201).

brief remarks (4:10–20) with other material Paul had sent to the Philippians (1:1–4:9, 4:21–23). In the three-letter theory, the order of sending would have been the letter of thanks (4:10–20), then months later the basic letter to the Philippians (1:1–3:1; 4:2–9, 21–23), and sometime still later the warning against the Judaizers (3:2–4:1).

However, these separations are artificial and unnecessary, as the commentary will show. The letter in its canonical form makes perfectly good literary sense as it stands. Rather than reading 3:1–4:1 as an interpolation, a better explanation is that Paul, while writing, was interrupted by news of the arrival of the Judaizers in Philippi and felt a need to address the serious situation immediately. Thus he changed his tack and began his diatribe against these dangerous heretics in 3:1b. Also, regarding 4:10–20, there is ample evidence in ancient friendship letters that the penning of thanks for gifts was often reserved for the end of the letter. Moreover, there is no evidence whatsoever that this letter ever existed without the passages of 3:1–4:1 and 4:10–20. It evidently has always been transmitted in the form in which we have it. Thus we conclude that this letter is an integrated whole as it appears in the canon.

AUTHORSHIP AND DATE

While there are many doubters regarding Paul's authorship of Colossians and Ephesians (see those commentaries within this series), the majority of commentators today agree that Paul wrote Philippians. Paul names himself as author (1:1), and the church fathers all listed the letter as Pauline. The personal details of the letter match closely what we know of the apostle, and the style and language are in keeping with those of other letters accepted as genuine. Details about Paul's imprisonment, the trial situation, and the establishment of the church in Philippi all fit the historical setting of the early 60s AD. Therefore we can confidently conclude that Paul wrote this letter.

The situation and date of writing are closely intertwined. Paul was arrested in Jerusalem on his final trip there following his third missionary journey (Acts 21) in approximately AD 57. There followed his two-year imprisonment in Caesarea, his trial before Festus and Agrippa (Acts 25–26), his voyage to Rome (Acts 27), and his two-year trial in Rome in AD 60–62 (Acts 28). Paul likely wrote Colossians and Ephesians midway through that period (AD 61) and Philippians at the end of that time (AD 62), based on his comments in Philippians 1:19–26, 2:23–24 that he expected to hear the verdict soon and hoped to be released. There has been debate as to whether this was the imprisonment in Ephesus (Acts 19:35–41; 1 Cor 15:32), Philippi (Acts 16:19–34), Caesarea (Acts 23:23–26:32), or Rome (Acts 28). As discussed in the commentaries on Colossians and Ephesians, the circumstances in the first three imprisonments do not fit well with what we actually see in the Prison Letters,[2] and the Roman trial provides by far the closest parallels. Therefore we can conclude that Philippians was written toward the end of Paul's trial in Rome in AD 62.

CIRCUMSTANCES AND CITY

Paul's labor in Philippi was a major milestone in his life, for this was the first city the apostle would have reached in the Grecian lands where he ministered. It took the vision from the man of Macedonia (Acts 16:6–10) to get him there. The city had been named after Phillip II, the father of Alexander the Great, and it was located on a major trade route called the Egnatian Way. However, it did not become important until 42 BC, when Mark Antony and Julius Caesar's nephew Octavian defeated Cassius and Brutus (the assassins of Julius Caesar) on a battlefield near the city. In honor of that victory, Octavian made Philippi a Roman colony and a settlement for veteran officers and soldiers. Considered a

---

2. The Prison Letters include Colossians, Philemon, Ephesians, and Philippians, all written during Paul's Roman imprisonment.

miniature copy of Rome itself, it became one of the region's leading cities, with about 10,000 inhabitants.

Philippi was a religiously diverse city, but it was home to few Jews, and there was a good deal of anti-Semitic prejudice that spilled over into persecution of the Christians. Apparently the residents' religious tolerance went only so far as to encompass variations on their own gods (Greco-Roman, Egyptian, Babylonian, etc.) and did not extend to the Judeo-Christian God.

Paul and his team (Silas, Timothy, and Luke) arrived in Philippi during the second missionary journey as they extended the gospel to Macedonia and Greece in about AD 50. They could not find a synagogue (implying that there were fewer than ten Jewish males in the city) and instead encountered a group of Jewish women and god-fearers meeting on the Sabbath for worship (Acts 16:13). Lydia, a wealthy god-fearer who sold expensive purple cloth, was the first convert and patron of the church established at Philippi (Acts 16:14-15, 40). Paul was forced to leave after the prison episode recorded in Acts 16:19-36, and as he finished that journey through Macedonia and Achaia the church in Philippi on several occasions helped the team financially (Phil 4:15-16). That church remained close to Paul for the rest of his ministry career. He probably revisited the believers there during the three-month stay in Macedonia and Achaia (Acts 20:1-3) on his way to Jerusalem.

During the tumultuous events following Paul's arrest in Jerusalem and his imprisonments, first in Caesarea (two years) and then in Rome (two years), the Philippians were unable to help him (4:10). But for some reason they found an opportunity to do so partway through his second year in Rome (while Paul was still incarcerated) and sent not only financial aid but a personal assistant, Epaphroditus (2:25-30) to help Paul in his ministry. This was incredibly encouraging, and one of the reasons Paul sent this letter was to pour out his love and gratitude for the Philippians' faithfulness.

PAUL'S PURPOSE AND THE PHILIPPIANS' OPPONENTS

Paul had four primary purposes for writing this letter:

1. To express his gratitude—As stated above, Paul was truly grateful for the Philippians' gift and wanted to thank them profusely (4:10-20). In itself, the theme of gratitude for the support of other believers is an important contribution to us. In his letters Paul often expresses thanksgiving to God and speaks about the gift of hospitality to others. This letter blends both into a lovely treatise on the Christian response of gratitude to others for their loving concern.

2. To report about his situation—Paul was excited about the success of his mission in Rome in spite of his seemingly impossible situation (1:12-14) and wanted to share with the Philippians not only this news but also news regarding his trial and the end that was in sight (1:19-26). He wanted them to share in the triumph of the gospel in the midst of seemingly insurmountable adversity.

3. To provide encouragement—Paul wanted to offer the Philippians consolation for the persecution and suffering they had been experiencing. The anti-Semitic and anti-Christian Macedonians had brought intense persecution upon the church, and Paul reminds the Philippian believers of God's will that they "not only believe on him but suffer for him" (1:29). Christ is the model of humility in suffering (2:8), Paul endures suffering as a sacrifice to God (2:17), and Epaphroditus demonstrates perseverance in suffering (2:26-27).

4. To provide instruction—Paul wanted to warn the Philippians about two significant problems: dissension in their church (2:1-18) and the appearance of false teachers (3:2-3, 17-18).

This fourth purpose involves major debate over the identity of those who were causing trouble among the Philippian believers.

While a few interpreters have tried to isolate a single group of opponents, that scenario is unlikely; it is best to recognize at least three and perhaps four separate groups of opponents mentioned in the letter.[3]

The first would be the preachers who were using their opportunity to promote the gospel to oppose Paul (1:15–17). They were definitely believers, for Paul rejoiced in them even though they were "stir[ring] up trouble" for him, because they were still preaching Christ faithfully. The second group includes Roman citizens and unbelievers who were persecuting the saints and frightening many (1:27–30). They cannot have been the same as any of the other groups because the others were problematic from inside the church, while the source of this trouble lay outside. The third group is the Judaizers, who believed that a Gentile had to convert to Judaism and observe the Mosaic law when coming to Christ (3:2–3; see also Galatians). The potential fourth group, mentioned at 3:18–19, is more difficult to identify. For most of my teaching career I held that there was a single group behind 3:2–3 and 3:18–19 (so three groups total), but as I re-examined the issue in writing this commentary I have changed my mind.

When taken at face value, Paul's remarks in 3:19 ("their god is their stomach, and their glory is in their shame") do not seem to fit a Jewish orientation for these opponents. Nevertheless, some interpreters—including myself, until recently—believe the Judaizers are still Paul's target here, based on reading verse 19 with a heavy dose of irony. In verse 2, Paul calls the Judaizers "dogs"; this epithet was used by Jews to label Gentiles unclean, but Paul flips it around, implying that the *Judaizers* were in fact the unclean ones because they had replaced the cross with circumcision as the basis of salvation. Paul also calls the Judaizers

---

3. For a more detailed discussion of the four groups I mention here, see the commentary on the cited passages.

"mutilators," a sarcastic twist on their agenda of circumcising Gentile Christians. In light of these remarks in verse 2 (so the theory goes), Paul could be doing something similar in verse 19, referring with irony to Jewish food laws ("their god is their stomach") and circumcision ("their glory is in their shame").

While this reading remains viable for some interpreters, I now regard it as too much of a stretch. As we will see in the commentary, the imagery in 3:18–19 seems to be referring directly to Gentiles (rather than indirectly to Jews), making it more plausible that Paul is describing a group different from the Judaizers. The data suggest a group of Gentile converts who were proto-**gnostics**[4] following a libertine, sensual lifestyle (similar to the false teachers in 1 John). So I find it probable that verses 2–3 refer to Judaizers and verses 18–19 to Gentile libertines, making four sets of opponents in all.

STRUCTURE AND OUTLINE

Philippians is straightforward when it comes to structural development. Paul is addressing the issues one at a time without using complicated organizational devices like **chiasm** (an A-B-B'-A' pattern) or recapitulation (cycles repeating material several times, as in 1 John or Revelation). His material is presented according to the following outline:

I. Greeting and prayer, 1:1–11
 A. Greeting to the church, 1:1–2
 B. Thanksgiving for their sharing in his ministry, 1:3–8
  1. His joy in their partnership, 1:3–5
  2. His confidence in God's work among them, 1:6
  3. His deep affection for them, 1:7–8

---

4. Full-blown **Gnosticism** (the belief in salvation via knowledge of secret truths) did not appear until the second century, but there were beginning stages in the first century, and this group could have represented one of them.

    C. Prayer for their spiritual growth, 1:9-11

       1. Prayer for overflowing love, 1:9

       2. Prayer for discernment of what is best, 1:10a

       3. Prayer for blameless lives, 1:10b

       4. Prayer for the fruit of righteousness, 1:11

II. The state of Paul and the gospel in Rome, 1:12-26

    A. Paul's chains—advancing the gospel, 1:12-14

       1. The results for his imprisonment in Rome, 1:12-13

       2. The results for Christian mission, 1:14

    B. The advance of the gospel in spite of impure motives, 1:15-18a

       1. Two motives for proclaiming Christ, 1:15-16

       2. Some out of love for Paul, 1:16

       3. Others out of ill will, 1:17

       4. The important consideration—proclaiming Christ, 1:18a

    C. Paul's situation: on trial for his life, 1:18b-26

       1. The possible outcomes—both would glorify Christ, 1:18b-20

         a. Joy in his deliverance, 1:18b-19

         b. The true goal—the glory of Christ, 1:20

       2. The difficult choice—life or death, 1:21-24

         a. The options—both desirable, 1:21

         b. The choices enumerated, 1:22-24

           1) To go on living would mean fruitful labor, 1:22

           2) To depart and be with Christ would be far better, 1:23

           3) To remain would be better for the Philippians, 1:24

       3. The joyous expectation—Paul would remain with them, 1:25-26

III. Call for unity at Philippi, 1:27–2:18

    A. Steadfastness and unity in the midst of persecution, 1:27–30

        1. The proper conduct—worthy of the gospel, 1:27–28

            a. Steadfast, united, and fearless, 1:27–28a

            b. The two signs—destruction and salvation, 1:28b

        2. The gift of suffering, 1:29–30

            a. The goal of suffering—for Paul, 1:29

            b. The model for the struggle—Paul, 1:30

    B. Humility in the midst of dissension, 2:1–4

        1. Four Christian experiences, 2:1

        2. Four needed internal qualities, 2:2

        3. The primary need for humility, 2:3–4

    C. Christ Jesus, the model for humility, 2:5–11

        1. Emulate the mindset of Christ, 2:5

        2. Christ's incarnation as the paradigm for humility, 2:6–11

            a. Christ's state of humiliation, 2:6–8

                1) His state of mind, 2:6

                2) His state of being—made himself nothing, 2:7

                3) His humility and crucifixion, 2:8

            b. Christ's state of exaltation, 2:9–11

                1) His exaltation by God, 2:9

                2) His exaltation by worship and submission, 2:10

                3) His exaltation by confession, 2:11

    D. Call to obedience, harmony, and purity, 2:12–18

        1. The demand for obedience, 2:12–13

            a. Their part: Working out their salvation, 2:12

            b. God's part: Working in them, 2:13

        2. The path of harmony and purity, 2:14–16a

            a. The refusal to complain and argue, 2:14

1) Everything loss to know Christ, 3:8a

2) Everything garbage to gain Christ, 3:8b–9a

3) The true gain—righteousness based on faith, 3:9b

 c. The true goal—to know Christ, 3:10–11

  1) The content—to know him, his resurrection, and his sufferings, 3:10a

  2) The means—to be like him in his death, 3:10b

  3) The goal—to attain his resurrection, 3:11

B. Perseverance amid worldly adversaries, 3:12–21

 1. The need to press on toward the goal, 3:12–16

  a. The key: Ongoing spiritual growth, 3:12–14

   1) Taking stock and forging ahead, 3:12

   2) The method for reaching the goal, 3:13–14

  b. Overcome differences with a mature mindset, 3:15–16

   1) For the less mature: God will clear up confusion, 3:15

   2) For the mature: Live up to what you have attained, 3:16

 2. The need to live not for the earthly but for the heavenly, 3:17–21

  a. Paul's living example, 3:17

  b. The indictment of worldly false teachers, 3:18–19

   1) Their designation—enemies of the cross, 3:18

   2) Four characteristics of the enemies, 3:19

  c. The true believers and their heavenly destiny, 3:20–21

   1) Citizenship in heaven, 3:20a

   2) Eager expectation—the glorious body awaiting, 3:20b–21

VI. Closing exhortations, 4:1–9
  A. Appeal for steadfastness and unity, 4:1–3
    1. Stand firm against false teachers, 4:1
    2. Find unity in the midst of conflict—Euodia and Syntyche, 4:2–3
  B. Calling them to joy and peace, 4:4–7
    1. Constant rejoicing, 4:4
    2. Known for their gentleness, 4:5
    3. Prayer, the antidote for anxiety, 4:6–7
      a. The means—prayer replacing worry, 4:6
      b. The result—the peace of God, 4:7
  C. The Christian mindset, 4:8–9
    1. Right thinking—excellent and praiseworthy things, 4:8
    2. Right doing—what they have learned from Paul, 4:9
VII. Thanksgiving for their generous gift, 4:10–20
  A. Thanks for the renewal of their concern, 4:10–13
    1. Recognizing their concern, 4:10
    2. Contentment in every circumstance, 4:11–12
    3. Christ, the source of strength, 4:13
  B. Thanks for their partnership in his ministry, 4:14–17
    1. Sharing in his difficulties, 4:14
    2. None shared but the Philippians, 4:15–16
    3. His desire—all this credited to their account, 4:17
  C. Thanks for their fragrant offering, 4:18–20
    1. The abundance of their acceptable sacrifice, 4:18
    2. The reward—God meeting all their needs, 4:19
    3. Doxological closing, 4:20
VIII. Final greetings, 4:21–23
  A. Request that they greet every saint, 4:21a
  B. Greeting from coworkers and saints in Rome, 4:21b–22
  C. Closing benediction, 4:23

THE THEOLOGY OF
THE LETTER

THE DOCTRINE OF CHRIST

As in virtually all of Paul's letters, Christ is the focal point of theological thought. Throughout the Prison Letters Paul centers on the exalted Lord, but Philippians, due to the Christ-hymn of 2:6-11, begins with the incarnation and sacrificial death of Christ. There is a strong emphasis here on Jesus' deity and pre-existent glory. The point is that his exaltation was not a new thing but rather a return to the glory of his pre-existent past. At his incarnation he surrendered his glory and "made himself nothing," coming as a slave to serve humankind. The emphasis is on Jesus' humility as the paradigm for us, and Paul's message is the definition of a godly person: one who, like Jesus, seeks humility and leaves the glory to God.

Christ is at the apex of every part of this letter. The final goal of every believer is to "know him" (3:8, 10), and everything in life worth having is ours "in Christ." Our task is to consider everything else loss—even garbage—to gain what really matters, Christ (3:7-9). His death on the cross (2:8) makes salvation possible, and the gospel being proclaimed to the world (see below) is the "gospel of Christ" (1:27). Gaining salvation comes through "faith in Christ," causing us to be "found in him" (3:9). We do not save ourselves; rather, Christ "takes hold of" us (3:12). In short, Christ is "God of very God" (as in the Nicene Creed)—the One who surrendered his glory to become our slave in order to bring us to God, and who is our model of humility, exemplifying for us the humble life that is pleasing to God.

THE GOSPEL OF CHRIST

Euangelion ("gospel") appears in Philippians nine times, making this letter tied with Romans for the most occurrences of *euangelion* in Paul's letters. Paul defines his ministry as "defending and confirming the gospel" (1:7), and his life's goal, including the results of his trial, is to "advance the gospel" (1:12). His joy in the Philippians is only somewhat based on their generous gift, stemming far more from their "partnership in the gospel" (1:5) — that glorious fellowship in which they, with Paul, proclaim God's truths to the world. For him everything in life must serve the gospel and God's will to bring salvation to a sinful world and return God's wandering creation to himself.

The gospel is the "good news of Christ" (v. 27a), that wondrous truth that in Christ sinners can be justified and reconciled to God. Paul defines the Christian life as walking in a way "worthy of the gospel of Christ," accomplished by "standing firm in the one spirit" through the "faith of the gospel" (v. 27b). To be the people of the gospel is to belong to God the Father, to believe in and follow God the Son, and to be guided and empowered by God the Spirit (v. 19; 2:1; 3:3).

THE CHURCH OF CHRIST

"In Christ," the dominant theme of the Prison Letters (appearing twenty-one times in Philippians alone), refers to those who as believers are united with Christ and as a result have become members of his body, the church. This oneness is first vertical with Christ and then horizontal with other believers. The church is the community of Christlike followers who experience corporate solidarity in him.

In Philippians, the main thing that defines believers "in Christ" is their rejection of everything the world offers in order to know and gain Christ (3:7–9). They do this by gaining the mindset of Christ (2:5) and by focusing both their thinking and their doing on the noble and pure aspects of Christ (3:8–9). In this way the Philippians have become "partners" with Paul and entered a "fellowship of the gospel" (one of the meanings of 1:5) as they together join him in the ministry of the gospel of Christ.

A major problem in a church defined by oneness is conflict. Infighting destroys a church's credibility with non-Christians, and believers are called to "shine like stars" with the light of God, the gospel (2:15). The answer to such bickering is simple yet quite difficult to attain—like-mindedness and mutual love (v. 2) fueled by a humility that is concerned for the other rather than the self (vv. 3–4). When God's people are characterized by loving concern and empowered by the Spirit to achieve a lasting fellowship (v. 1), the church truly becomes the community of Christ.

The Christian walk is the defining characteristic of the messianic community. Their "citizenship is in heaven" (3:20), not earth, and they are to live accordingly. As they strive with all they have to attain the heavenly goal (vv. 13–14) of Christlikeness, they will gain "the fruit of righteousness" (1:11) and find peace and joy in the midst of all the troubles that come their way (v. 27; 4:6–7). Life will always contain suffering, especially for God's people (1:29), but the church of Christ will learn to persevere, to walk in Christ through the pitfalls of life, and to triumph over all adversity and affliction. The way to do this is to realize that joy comes not through external circumstances in life but through an internal relationship with the Triune Godhead. God will ultimately reverse all hardships and repay all sacrifices, and when we depend on him through prayer his peace triumphs over the thunderous clamor life throws at us.

THE RETURN OF CHRIST

Philippians does not center on the second coming of Christ and the end of history to the extent of, say, James or 1 Peter, but this is still a major concern of the book. Paul speaks frequently of the "day of Christ" as the completion of God's work among us (1:6), the goal of our Christian living (v. 10), and the time when he will answer to Christ for the quality of his ministry (2:16). Moreover, our present life is lived in terms of our upward call to live in light of his parousia/return (3:14), when we will be transformed to be like him (v. 21).

Paul strongly emphasizes the paired realities of the "already" and the "not yet,"[5] meaning that the believer has already begun to receive all the promises of Scripture but has not yet received them fully. We are living in the time of fulfillment, and our task is to press on in the race God has set before us to receive the prize he has for us (3:12–14; see also Heb 12:1–3). This truth regarding the purpose of the present time in God's plan transforms for us the issue of trials and suffering. The critical aspect is no longer the question of present pain but the certainty of future glory. God is transcendent over evil, and we as his people are too. We turn our backs on the past (3:13) and turn present problems into future promise. At present our bodies are frail and "lowly," but in Christ we know that in this frailty we are "like him in his death" (v. 10) and that we will soon be transformed to be like him in his glory (v. 21).

---

5. The technical term for this is "inaugurated **eschatology**," referring to the New Testament view that the last days have begun in the first coming of Christ but will not be consummated until his second coming.

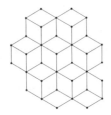

GREETING AND PRAYER FOR LOVE AND DISCERNMENT
(1:1–11)

All of Paul's letters follow Hellenistic letter-writing conventions by beginning with a greeting, a thanksgiving, and a prayer for the recipients' well-being. However, Paul always goes beyond the conventional by turning the opening prayer into an introduction to the letter's contents. He is praying that God will bless what he has to say to the Philippians. Greek letters tend to be short and stereotyped in these matters, but Paul extends these elements and turns them into a theological tour-de-force that becomes almost a table of contents for the message of the letter. He stresses servanthood and the Philippians' partnership in the gospel, along with their close relationship to himself, and also reflects on his situation as a prisoner in Rome. Then he asks God to give them a deeper love and a greater discernment into the path of discipleship in Christ. All of this leads into the rest of the letter.

PAUL GREETS THE PHILIPPIAN CHRISTIANS (1:1–2)

The order here (author, recipient, and greetings) was common first-century practice. In this setting the apostle uses his Greek name, "Paul," rather than his Hebrew name, "Saul," to relate to his readers. Though Paul is the true author of this letter (he uses "I" throughout), he adds Timothy here (as in 2 Cor 1:1; Col 1:1; Phlm 1), probably because Timothy was serving as an **amanuensis** (or secretary) and Paul dictated the letter due to his own poor eyesight (see Gal 6:11; Col 4:18). Timothy was also an important assistant and member of Paul's ministry team. As a young man he had joined Paul's team at the beginning of the second missionary journey (Acts 16:1-4) and had been a close associate and friend ever since (see the commendation in Phil 2:19-24). The Philippians had probably become close to Timothy during the missionaries' stay in Philippi (Acts 16:11-40), so Paul wanted them to know that Timothy had a part in this letter.

Paul uncharacteristically declines to emphasize his own identity as an apostle but instead chooses to label both Timothy and himself as "servants (Greek: *douloi*, which is better translated 'slaves') of Christ Jesus." The primary aspect of the slave metaphor for first-century readers was belonging, with servanthood a secondary thrust. Slaves were owned by their master and completely under his control. Paul wanted the Philippians to know the true lordship of God and Christ. He himself was not in charge but served his Master and Lord, Christ, and belonged to him lock, stock, and barrel. Romans 6 says it well: God redeemed us from enslavement to sin so that we could become his slaves (for example, Rom 6:22). We exchanged an evil, abusive taskmaster for a loving, caring master who watches over and protects us. For Israel as well as for the church, then, slavery was a precious metaphor; in the case of the church it powerfully depicts our redemption or purchase by God and then emphasizes the importance of our surrender and obedience to God and Christ. All the great men and women of God in the Old Testament (like Abraham, Moses, and David) called themselves slaves of God— an honored designation of subservience and belonging.

Still, Paul's choice to use the term here also emphasizes the servanthood aspect. Based on Philippians 2:1-3 it is possible that there was a power struggle going on among the leaders at Philippi. Such a conflict would have brought dissension into the life of the church, so Paul wanted to model servanthood leadership for them. Their master was clear—"Christ Jesus," named three times in these first two verses to leave no doubt as to who was truly in charge. Christ is Lord of all, and our primary duty is to obey and emulate him in everything we do. All the problems Paul discusses in this letter were due to their failure to live out these divine directives to make Christ their Lord and Master.

The recipients were "all God's people [literally, 'saints'] in Christ Jesus at Philippi" (v. 2). Paul frequently addresses his recipients as "saints" (1 and 2 Cor 1:1; Rom 1:1; Eph 1:2; Col 1:2) or "holy ones," one of the primary titles in the New Testament for those called to live as "set apart" from the world for God. God had chosen them to belong to himself and set them apart to be his special people. This is another title of honor, and together with "slave" it indicated that they were God's special possession, called to a sacred task in serving and living for him.

These holy people are once again described as being "in Christ Jesus," emphasizing their new identity as the messianic community. The "in Christ" motif is dominant in the Prison Letters (Colossians, Philemon, Ephesians, and Philippians) and emphasizes union with Christ and membership in his body, the church. To be in him is to belong to him, to be one with him, and to be part of his people. Our residence is in Christ, and since we are his, we focus on him in all we do and live every moment as Christ-people. Paul pairs this christological identification with the believers' geographical identity as residents of Philippi (for details about the city's background, see the introduction).

An unusual feature is the added "together with the overseers and deacons," offices Paul mentions elsewhere only in the Pastoral Letters (for example, 1 Tim 3:1, 2, 8, 12). Many critical scholars believe that the churches Paul founded had no hierarchy of leaders until late in the first century, but Acts makes it clear that "elders" functioned almost from the beginning (Acts 11:30; 14:23; 15:2, 4, 6, and others), and there is little reason to doubt the historicity of these passages. The early church would naturally have followed Jewish patterns in this area, as they did in worship and church life. So this was not a later development but existed virtually from the beginning.

Interestingly, these church officers are not mentioned anywhere else in this letter. So why here? Note that the reference is actually to "all the saints along with the bishops and deacons," followed by thanks to them for their "partnership in the gospel" (v. 5). Toward the end of the letter, in 4:14–18, the specifics are noted. They have "shared" or partnered with Paul by sending him gifts carried by Epaphroditus, whom they sent specifically to help Paul in his ministry (2:25–30). So Paul is thanking the leaders as well as the whole church for their generosity and help. He might also have been singling out these leaders because he wanted them to carry out his instructions, specifically with regard to the persecution they were enduring (1:27–30), the dissension in the church (2:1–3, 12–18; 4:2–3), and the appearance of false teachers in their midst (3:1–4:1).

The "overseers" or "bishops" were those charged with "watching over" or administering the church. Both in Acts (20:28) and in the Pastorals (1 Tim 3:2; Titus 1:7) elders are seen as carrying out this function.[1] The idea is supervision, oversight, and pastoral care. The "deacon" image stems from the first-century household servant (Greek: *diakonos*) and likely describes those who served the church in practical ministry (Rom 16:1; 1 Tim 3:8), though the term was also used generally to refer to "ministers" in the church (Col 1:7; 1 Thess 3:2). Here these terms likely refer to those church officers who sent the gifts to Paul and whom he trusted to carry out his instructions and solve the serious problems at Philippi.

---

1. Elders also carry out the pastoral office. The three terms ("elder," "overseer," and "pastor") appear to be synonymous in the New Testament.

The greeting itself (v. 2) is standard in Paul's letters. The Greek greeting "grace" (*charis*) and the Hebrew greeting "peace" (*shalom*) are not only combined here but are infused with Christian content. The qualities both Greeks and Jews wanted from life (grace and peace) were now offered them in Christ by God. Paul often stresses the Fatherhood of God in his greetings, because the saints have become the children of God through adoption (Rom 8:14–17) and now have a loving Father who cares for them and is involved deeply in their lives. Note also that this greeting does not come merely from "Christ" but from "the Lord Jesus Christ." There is great emphasis in Philippians on the exaltation of Christ after he sacrificed himself on the cross (2:9–11), and Paul frequently emphasizes his lordship or sovereignty over this world (fifteen times in this letter). The sacrificial Lamb has become the exalted Lord.

PAUL THANKS THEM FOR SHARING IN HIS MINISTRY (1:3–8)

HIS JOY IN THEIR PARTNERSHIP (1:3–5)

Greek letters commonly included a brief and stylized wish for the well-being of the friend to whom the letter was being sent. Paul Christianizes this convention and turns it into a genuine prayer of thanksgiving, and it has a twofold purpose—praise for the good relationship Paul has with the Philippians and an introduction to major theme(s) that will come up in the letter. Paul has been especially close to this church, and they more than any other believers have kept up with Paul and been involved in his ministry from the time they got to know him. So at the beginning and end of this letter (1:3; 4:18) Paul makes it a point to thank them for the gifts they have sent him.

Three aspects of prayer are combined here—intercession, thanksgiving, and joy—all focused on the Philippians. But note that Paul is thankful not only to them; "I thank my God" acknowledges that the gift has actually come from God through them.

They have been a channel through whom God has taken care of Paul. So the primary focus is God, but still Paul is extremely grateful for the Philippians, who have allowed themselves to be used by God to care for his needs.

There are two ways the next phrase can be read: It could center on their gift ("for your every remembrance of me") or on Paul's reminiscences ("every time I remember you"). The Greek could read either way, but everywhere else Paul uses this phrase (Rom 1:9; Eph 1:16; 1 Thess 1:2, 3:6; 2 Tim 1:3; Phlm 4) it refers to himself, and that is likely the case here as well. Paul often thought of the Philippians' concern and generosity, and this led in every instance to thanksgiving. Paul was a prayer warrior, and an essential part of that regular prayer was thanksgiving.

Moreover, Paul was a general optimist who dwelled on the positives, and as such he adds in verse 4 three further aspects of his prayer life:

1. Its frequency—Thanksgiving, Paul says, takes place "in all my prayers" as an ongoing response to his deep friendship with this church. It must be understood that "always" (Greek: *pantote*) does not mean unceasingly but rather denotes in this context regular prayer. Remembering the Philippians was a part of his daily prayer life.

2. Its focus—His prayer was regularly "for all of you." He kept the Philippians always in his mind and heart and so prayed for each one as often as he could. Paul was more than a general prayer warrior; he was a *personal* prayer warrior who frequently brought the members of this congregation and their needs to God's attention.

3. The joy with which he prayed—Even though the church of Philippi had many problems, as we will see, Paul was filled with joy as he reflected on the many good things God was doing among them and on all the good they were doing for him. The grace note of joy reverberates through the letter, surfacing fourteen times; it was the primary emotion

Paul felt when he thought of these believers, and that is reflected in his prayers. The Christian life is by definition a life of joy, but often individual situations are filled with grief and pain (Heb 12:11). However, when we recognize the sovereign hand of God in our lives (Rom 8:28) all trials lead to joy (Jas 1:2; 1 Pet 1:6). This is how Paul felt about the Philippians. He experienced sorrow when he reflected on their problems (3:18) but rejoiced because God was in charge of even these painful areas.

In verse 5 we find the particular reason for Paul's joy on this occasion—"your partnership in the gospel." He uses a well-known Greek word, *koinōnia*, that connotes a deep-seated "fellowship," as well as a sharing in an enterprise. So he was rejoicing that the Philippian believers had partnered with him in proclaiming the gospel in their area and had shared in his own ministry of proclamation through their support, both via financial giving and in their personal prayers and encouragement. Theirs was a twofold fellowship with Paul: they partnered with him both in his ministry and in their own ministry of sharing the good news of Christ (see my comments on v. 7, below).

PAUL'S CONFIDENCE IN GOD'S WORK AMONG THEM (1:6)

Paul's joy in every situation was based on a deep-seated confidence in God, a realization that "he who began a good work in you will carry it on to completion until the day of Jesus Christ." This is why adverse circumstances and sorrows could not deter the basic joy with which Paul approached life. Yes, the Philippian church was dealing with dissension, many of its members were enduring severe persecution, and false teachers were threatening its stability. However, Paul totally trusted that the Lord of the universe remained in charge and that he and his love would never desert them (Rom 8:31, 35, 39). So his indefatigable joy was grounded in his indestructible confidence in God.

God's good work (see 2:13) in their midst had begun with the arrival of the gospel and had led first to their conversion and then to the work of the Spirit in their lives. It embraced the spiritual growth of the people, their life of sanctification, and their partnership in the gospel. God's good work included the suffering they had experienced, for it constituted a "fellowship of suffering" with Christ (3:10), as well as with Paul. They were pressured both from outside (1:28) and from inside (4:2-3) their church, but through it all God was at work, and the end result was guaranteed because they knew he would "carry it to completion"—would bring it to the God-intended end his will had determined. We too can know that our final victory is completely certain so long as we rely on God, for the future is entirely in his hands. We fail only when we forget that reality and try to run our own lives.

This good work of God on our behalf will continue "until the day of Jesus Christ," the end of history and the beginning of eternity. When God created the universe, he knew the fall would occur and determined that he would have to personally enter this world and pay the price for our sins so we could be redeemed. So the beginning of this world already awaited its end, when that redemption would be complete and evil would once and for all time be destroyed. The same is true with our individual lives. God is watching over and preparing us for that day when Christ returns and this world ends. He is ever vigilant, so his good work on our behalf is unceasing (Rom 8:31-39). Our responsibility is to surrender completely to him and to determine that at all times we will rely on his strength rather than on our own (Eph 6:10-12).

His Deep Affection for Them (1:7-8)

Paul's expression of thanksgiving is finished, and so he reminisces briefly about his deep affection for the Philippian church, saying, "It is right for me to feel this way about all of you," a reference to the deep-seated joy he felt[2] every time he thought of them. This church more than any other had stayed solidly behind Paul, supporting him throughout his ordeal. It is difficult for us to imagine all that he had to endure. We tend to get upset every time some little thing goes wrong, even to the point of accusing God of abandoning us. When Paul went to Jerusalem on that last trip after the third missionary journey (Acts 20–21), he had wonderful plans for switching his ministry to the western half of the Roman Empire (Rom 15:23–29) and for completing his life's mission as apostle to the Gentiles. Those plans went awry, and he spent the next four years in limbo—and in prison, first in Caesarea (Acts 24–26) and then in Rome. While many deserted Paul, the Philippians did not; they went so far, in fact, as to send Epaphroditus to be his personal assistant (Phil 2:25–30). No other church remained as faithful and true as this one, and Paul's heart was warmed every time he thought of them. So he wanted these close friends to realize how right and proper it was for him to retain this joyous attitude toward them. Philippians is, in essence, a "friendship letter."

Paul relates two reasons for his joyous feelings. First, "I have you in my heart," a declaration showing the depth of his feelings for them. Paul, in Rome, may have been separated from them both by a great physical distance and by an even more difficult situation (he was on trial for his life), but nothing could dampen his great love for these faithful friends. Friendship is a precious commodity, and Paul more than any of us (being that he was in danger of an imminent death sentence) needed close companions.

Second, the Philippians partnered/shared (as in 1:5, koinōnia: "fellowship") with him through thick and thin. This

---

2. The Greek word *phronein* refers to the mindset as well as to feelings, and thus to the times the Philippians came to Paul's mind and the feelings this awakened in his heart. The same word is used in 2:5 for "*have the same mindset as Christ Jesus.*"

deep fellowship was "in God's grace," but it is difficult to determine what "grace" Paul had in view. It could have been the saving grace of God or Paul's apostolic calling as God's grace-gift (Rom 12:3; Gal 2:9); certainly the Philippians shared in both with Paul. But in this context it is more likely that they were sharing in his current situation of suffering, in the "fellowship of suffering" (3:10) he describes in 1:29–30—"it has been granted to you … not only to believe in him, but also to suffer for him … the same struggle you saw I had." So Paul meant that God had "graciously" given them the privilege of sharing in his struggle through their prayers and giving.

Paul identifies two specific areas in this struggle. First, through their gifts they have shared in Paul's "chains," both a metaphor for Paul's imprisonment in general and literally true since Paul likely was chained to a Roman guard most of the time. The fact that he stresses his "chains" three more times in verses 13, 14, and 17 exemplifies his frustration with this aspect of his situation. Imagine writing this entire letter with a chain connecting your wrist to that of a Roman guard. Paul had spent most of his adult life freely traveling from one place of ministry to another, and now for four years he had been restricted to a prison environment and chained regularly to guards.

Second, the Philippian believers shared with Paul in "defending and confirming the gospel," in one sense referring to the proclamation of gospel truth but more specifically here to his trial situation. These are legal terms describing a defense before a court of law. Paul would appear before the emperor, Nero, to defend himself against all charges and confirm his innocence. Yet he means more than this, because as in Caesarea in the trial before Festus and Agrippa (Acts 26) Paul would use this trial as an opportunity to present the gospel. The gifts of the Philippians helped make it possible for Paul to continue living in the apartment in Rome (Acts 28:30) and to use his time more for ministry than for legal matters. Paul relates the success of these efforts below in verses 12–13, noting with joy that his time in Rome has served to "advance the gospel ... throughout the whole palace guard and to everyone else."

He ends the thanksgiving with another emotional affirmation of his love for this church (v. 8). He is once again deeply moved and calls on God himself to "testify how I long for all of you." Here we see the intensity of his feelings for these close friends (in a real sense his BFFs). It was insufficient to declare his love for them; he wanted God to act as a witness. Paul was about to send Epaphroditus back, meaning that the one concrete presence in his life of the Philippian church would be gone and that all he would have left would be his memories.

This was almost a trinitarian longing, for God was his witness and the source of his affection is "Christ Jesus." "God is my witness," in fact, makes this an official oath; Paul was swearing an oath in the presence of God to affirm his deep longing for these friends (see 4:1). Moreover, he wanted them to know that it was not mere human feelings but "the affection of Christ Jesus" that was moving him. (The Greek word Paul uses here, *splanchna*, can refer literally to the "bowels" or figuratively to one's innermost feelings.) His love for the Philippians was a reflection of Christ's love for them. There could not have been a deeper statement of Paul's love and fellowship, and he wanted them to realize how intensely he longed to be with them. The word "all" appears three times in verses 7–8, showing that Paul did not want to leave out any believer, including even those who were causing the dissension he addresses in 2:1–18 or those influenced by the Judaizers in chapter 3. Paul wanted each individual member of this church to know how much he loved them.

PAUL PRAYS FOR THEIR SPIRITUAL GROWTH (1:9–11)

PRAYER FOR OVERFLOWING LOVE (1:9)

In verse 4 Paul spoke of his unceasing prayers for the Philippian believers. He now reveals the content of those prayers.

The depth of his love for them could only lead to intercessory prayer. Having just declared his deep "affection" for them, he now prays for their communal love for one another, that it may "abound more and more," experiencing limitless growth. The love that flowed from God and Christ to them and that was reflected in their relationship with Paul must now radiate throughout the community. The reason for this emphasis will become evident in 2:1–4 when Paul addresses the dissension and disunity that are threatening this church. This was normally a loving congregation, and while internal love within the community remained uppermost in his mind Paul undoubtedly had in mind every aspect of love—the love-relationship with God and Christ, the internal love within the congregation, and their external relationships with unbelievers ("love your neighbor," Lev 19:18). It was paramount that these believers make certain that this love did not stagnate but continued to grow (1 Thess 3:12). I would define this *agapē* love as "selfless giving," the opposite of the "selfish ambition" in 2:3 and the result of God's love transforming the worldly, sinful self.

The sphere within which communal love abounds is "knowledge and depth of insight." The underlying idea is 3:10, "I want to know Christ." Beyond intellectual comprehension, Paul had in view an experiential knowledge that begins with a living relationship with Christ. This is seen in his use of the Greek term *epignōsis*, which not only indicates the mental grasp of God's (and life's) truths, but also encompasses the concrete application of those truths in everyday living. "Depth of insight" (literally, "all insight") stresses the moral aspect and stems from Proverbs (where it appears twenty-seven times); the term connotes practical discernment of the right thing to do in a given situation (see also Col 1:9). So Paul wanted the Philippians' love to increase within the sphere of their experience of Christ's love. This would result in moral discernment regarding life in the community.

PRAYER FOR DISCERNMENT OF WHAT IS BEST (1:10A)

This verse actually relates two purposes of verse 9, as Paul prays for abounding love and insight "so that" the believers might be able to discern what is best and live pure lives. Life is controlled by choices, many of which can be less than beneficial for us. It is not always easy to distinguish the choices that might harm us, particularly in that they often appear more attractive and a lot more fun than the good ones. The word for "discern" (*dokimazein*) connotes testing a thing to ascertain its true value, as in 1 Peter 1:7 of gold "tested" by fire to prove its genuineness. Spiritual discernment will test the options to determine which will truly be for the best.

Often, in fact, our life choices include not only the obviously bad, but also nuances of the good, the better, and the best. For Paul a personal "good" might have entailed hunkering down in the safety of his hometown of Tarsus or even the relative security of his adopted city of Jerusalem, but the best option in terms of kingdom benefit lay in his life of near-continuous travel to "preach the gospel where Christ was not known" (Rom 15:20). On that last trip to Jerusalem his companions begged him to opt for the good, to avoid Jerusalem and certain arrest (Acts 21:10–14), but Paul chose the best and went willingly to his lengthy imprisonment and the penning of his Prison Letters. For us, as well, the best will not always be easy or comfortable, but it will always produce eternal reward.

PRAYER FOR BLAMELESS LIVES (1:10B)

The second purpose of a discerning mind is spiritual and moral purity. In verse 6 Paul states his confidence that Christ would continue his work in the Philippian Christians "until the day of Christ Jesus," and now he prays that this work would enable them to live blameless lives and be ready for the Day of the Lord. This emphasis on the end of the age shows that Paul viewed human history as salvation history—that is, as a time during which the church must grow spiritually and prepare for eternity.

The Greek word for "pure" (*eilikrineis*), the positive aspect, means to be sincere, with untainted motives. The result of the deep love already discussed, the term defines a life without hypocrisy and dedicated to others rather than self. The negative aspect is "blameless" (*aproskopoi*), descriptive of a life that does not offend others or cause them to stumble. Taken together, Paul's point is that God's people are to test and discern the right thing to do at all times so that others will be strengthened and encouraged rather than turned away from Christ. On the last day we will all stand before God and give account for our lives; Paul wants these people to realize this and use their time wisely to prepare for that day.

Prayer for the Fruit of Righteousness (1:11)

This final request sums up the others, as each of these qualities—love, discernment, and blamelessness—constitutes a "fruit of righteousness" in their lives. Paul's prayer is that on the day when Christ returns he might find them "filled to the full" (*plēroō*) with the fruit of their righteous lives. He wants them to keep growing day by day so that at the end of the age Christ's work in them will have come to completion. God has planted them in his vineyard, and it is their task to grow into ripe, glorious fruit (Ps 1:3; Isa 5:1–4; John 15:1–8), ready for that final harvest that will usher in eternity (Matt 13:24–30, 36–43).

The fruit here would be linked with the fruit of the Spirit in Galatians 5:22–23 and the fruitful branches of John 15:1–8. "Righteousness" refers to the righteous work of God in our lives and our virtuous living that results. The picture here is of Christ producing his work ("that comes through Jesus Christ") in the church and its bearing fruit. There are three issues: (1) The emphasis is corporate rather than individual. The church as the body of

Christ is the focus of Christ's activity. Individuals, though obviously present, are members of Christ's body. (2) Paul's reference is to the process of sanctification or spiritual growth more than it is to redemption. The emphasis on the growth of the church is similar to the thrust in Ephesians 4:11–16, which depicts the church growing to maturity in Christ. (3) The stress is on the process of growth, as the emergent fruit first produces buds on the vine and then throughout the life of the church grows to maturity, to be completed on the Day of Christ when he returns. As in John 15 the picture is of Christ producing the nourishing sap (his righteous work) that enables the branch to bud and then to develop (righteous) fruit that ripens to maturity.

"Righteousness" has multiple meanings. It is the righteous power of the Godhead in our lives but even more the result of that work in us. Here we have the three stages of "righteousness" in Paul, seen especially in Romans 3:24. As a result of Christ's atoning sacrifice, God has declared us righteous in his eyes (justification) and then has begun the process by which he makes us righteous before himself (sanctification), the result of which is that we live righteously for him (ethical righteousness). All three may be intended here, but the third is the primary thrust. Paul challenges the Philippians to allow the power of Christ to bear righteous fruit in their lives and then to allow that fruit to grow exponentially and fill them to capacity as they get ready for Christ to end this world and launch eternity.

The purpose of all this is not their own reward but "the glory and praise of God." The second item of the Lord's Prayer is "Hallowed be your name," or "May your name be glorified" (Matt 6:9; Luke 11:2). In everything we do we are to seek not our own self-glory ("vain glory," Phil 2:3) but to glorify God with our life and activities. That should be our prayer every morning. As a teacher and preacher I pray this every time I proclaim God's word. In the prologue to Ephesians (1:3–14) this plea that God be praised occurs four times (vv. 3, 6, 12, 14). Every spiritual blessing we experience and everything we do is to have as its goal the praise of God's glory.

———

Paul begins every one of his letters with a loving greeting in Christ and, in most of them, proceeds to thank God and to pray for the letter's recipients. This is especially the case in Philippians, due to his extremely close relationship with the believers at Philippi. Paul has experienced their deep love personally but now prays that this love will increase and help them to overcome their problems—persecution, dissension, and false teaching. For us the solution is the same—to surrender wholeheartedly to Christ and to allow him to give us the love and spiritual discernment to overcome all obstacles and glorify him through our lives.

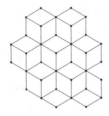

THE STATE OF PAUL AND THE GOSPEL IN ROME—PART I
(1:12–18a)

The first section was all about Paul's prayer concern for the Philippians. Now he wishes to inform them about his own current situation, as well as the progress of the gospel witness in Rome. This is undoubtedly due to the closeness he felt for these people. More than any other church, these friends had shown a loving concern for Paul and his situation, sending both a monetary gift and an assistant, Epaphroditus, to care for Paul himself. Paul responds with very good news indeed: Not only is he doing surprisingly well considering the trial situation (vv. 12-14) and the opposition he has faced from some ministers of the gospel (vv. 15-17), but the gospel itself has made miraculous inroads into the Roman governmental apparatus, as well as throughout the Roman empire (vv. 12-14). As for his trial, it was showing signs of coming to an end, one that Paul believed might possibly enable a personal visit to Philippi at some time in the future (vv. 20-26).

PAUL TELLS HOW HIS IMPRISONMENT
HAS ADVANCED THE GOSPEL (1:12-14)

THE RESULTS OF HIS IMPRISONMENT AMONG
ROMAN GUARDS AND OFFICIALS (1:12-13)

In typical Pauline style these verses form a single lengthy sentence and detail what he considered the single most important point, the advancement of the gospel through the very fact of his imprisonment. He employs a common formula in letters like this, addressing the readers ("brothers and sisters"), followed by an introductory comment regarding the news to come ("I want you to know"). First he relates how the gospel message is progressing within the governmental apparatus of Rome (v. 13) and then its progress outside official channels in the general Roman populace (v. 14). Moreover, not only is his own witness all the more effective, but the other believers in Rome are emboldened to proclaim Christ more directly and effectively. So the gospel is being advanced among unbelievers (v. 13) and is being promoted more boldly by believers (v. 14). Paul says nothing here about his personal circumstances, which were irrelevant, but centers on what really matters—the propagation of the gospel.

Paul's point is that in significant ways his arrest and capital trial have turned out to *enhance* the gospel and proclaim the name of Christ. The word "chains" occurs in both verses 13 and 14. Normally we would expect the prisoner to wax eloquent on the tragedy of the whole situation, the outrageous robbery of five years of his life and the injustice associated with the arrest of an innocent man. Paul relates none of that but instead centers on the joy of what God has done with the horrendous situation: "What has happened to me has actually served to advance the gospel." Many would see only the sorrow of his imprisonment, but Paul is saying that what has "really" occurred is quite different.

The circumstances Paul has had to endure these last several years have certainly been "painful" or grievous (Heb 12:11), but they have been for the best (Rom 8:28). It is clear that Paul would not have traded them for any other scenario, because God had turned everything around to accomplish exactly what Paul had wanted for his trip to Rome, to "have a harvest among you" (Rom 1:13), and that when he came he would arrive "in the full measure of the blessing of Christ" (Rom 15:29). That is exactly what had transpired, and in ways that could not have occurred in any other circumstances. Paul could never have reached the guards and other leaders if he had simply been a Jewish-Christian peasant preaching Christ on the streets of the city. God had used Paul's capital trial to accomplish a miracle! Paul now realized God's true intentions for all those years of his languishing in prison, and his amazement and joy are clear.

The first result (v. 13) is that "it has become clear throughout the whole palace guard and to everyone else that I am in chains for Christ." The actual order of the Greek is "my chains have become visible in Christ," signifying that "in Christ" modifies "become visible/clear" and not just "my chains." Paul is saying that his union with Christ has turned the whole situation around. The Romans might have thought he was Caesar's prisoner in chains, but Paul has made it evident to all that Christ was actually in charge, and that his shackles are in reality Christ's chains. He was in prison "because of Christ," and there is a double meaning in this: His witness for Christ had brought him to this point, yes, but more importantly Christ had orchestrated the entire situation for his own purposes.

However, Paul was not speaking generally about his trial situation but specifically about his witness to the guards and the other Roman officials he had encountered during his imprisonment. The "palace guard" or "Praetorian guard" oversaw the emperor's palace (the Praetorium) and governmental apparatus of Rome. They were the elite soldiers of the Roman Empire, nine thousand in number, and they oversaw everything that went on in Rome. The guards watching over Paul would have been regularly rotated, but even so he could not have conversed with a majority of them. Probably he is referring to word of mouth, in that the guards he did encounter told others about his circumstances and about his witness for Christ. Also, this is hyperbole, a literary device by which Paul is saying that his witness was known throughout the guard. The phrase "everyone else" most likely refers to other governmental officials—those called "Caesar's household" in 4:23—many of whom Paul would have met in the legal proceedings surrounding his trial. So the witness about Christ had circulated throughout Rome, especially in the inner circles of power. Paul's point was that his imprisonment had made all of this possible.

The Results of His Imprisonment for Christian Witness (1:14)

The rest of the Roman populace had been evangelized by the other Christians in Rome. Here we see the other result of Paul's imprisonment—its effect on the church. It is difficult to know whether Paul was speaking primarily of believers in Rome or more widely of those in the rest of the province of Asia and even throughout the Roman Empire who had heard of the effects of Paul's "chains." Still, since it is clear from the note here that the Philippians did not yet know this, Paul was primarily thinking of those in Rome itself. The term here rendered "confident" (*pepoithotas*) means to become "bold" or "fearless." When Paul arrived in Rome in chains, many Christians were likely paralyzed by the fear of a tsunami of persecution that might be coming, but when they saw the power of his witness and its effects on the Roman elite they must have thought, "If he can do this while on trial for his life, how much more should we be able to accomplish."

Their confidence was not in Paul but "in the Lord."[1] His example was the basis for their newfound courage to witness, but Christ was the true source of their boldness. Paul uses strong language here, as the empowering presence of the Lord through Paul's example had enabled the believers "all the more to proclaim the gospel without fear." There is a superlative force implied in Paul's phraseology, as their witness had become "all the more" bold and powerful. The Christians in Rome, who at one time cowered in fear, had broken free of that intimidation and found the courage to ignore the danger that they too could end up in prison. Ironically, Paul's imprisonment had made them ignore the possibility of their own incarceration and to "speak the word" with even greater power. The "word" (Greek: *logos*) in Paul always refers to the gospel truths about Christ, and that is the thrust here, as in the NIV's "proclaim the gospel." This is a message for us as well, for this "bold" witness is as needed today as it was in the first century.

THE GOSPEL ADVANCES IN SPITE OF IMPURE MOTIVES (1:15–18A)

TWO MOTIVES FOR PROCLAIMING CHRIST (1:15-16)

Among the "brothers and sisters" in the province (vv. 12, 14) there were conflicting attitudes toward Paul. He had always been a polarizing figure, first as the persecutor of the church and then as the missionary to the Gentiles. Conflict dogged his steps throughout his life, both outside the church and within it. Here the conflict was over Paul himself, not his message. Both factions were part of the Philippian church and clearly preached the same gospel, and that is Paul's main point. None of them were false teachers, Jewish opponents, or Roman persecutors. He was

---

1. Some versions (KJV, NLT) translate "brothers in the Lord," but in Paul the "in Christ" motif normally modifies the verb (so NRSV, NIV, NASB, ESV).

unconcerned about attitudes toward himself, so he rejoiced even in his opponents, so long as they continued to preach the gospel.

The first group, Paul contends, was preaching the gospel "out of envy and rivalry," two terms normally found in vice lists of sinful attitudes (for example, Rom 1:28-29; Gal 5:20-21; 1 Tim 6:3-4). Envy is a jealous attitude in which a person wants what another person has and wishes to deprive the other of what they feel they themselves rightfully deserve. Rivalry describes the result of envy, a divisive spirit that undermines the cohesiveness of the group and causes people to take sides. The result of the two is disunity and strife, those qualities that will destroy the mission of the church, which according to Jesus' high priestly prayer in John 17:20-23 is dependent on the unity of God's people.

The other group of preachers proclaims Christ "out of goodwill," in complete support of Paul and his leadership in the church. Many read this "goodwill" vertically and not just horizontally, encompassing the recognition of God's favor toward Paul. Often in Scripture the concept refers to God's pleasure in a person or thing, and that is likely Paul's thrust here, although both aspects appear to be in view. In contrast to the ill will of the negative faction, many church leaders were convinced that God's blessing lay on Paul and so gave him their support and favor.

SOME OUT OF LOVE FOR PAUL (1:16)

There is a chiastic arrangement in verses 15-17:

    A Some out of envy, 1:15a

      B Others out of goodwill, 1:15b

      B' Some out of love, 1:16

    A' Others out of selfish ambition, 1:17

The purpose of these verses is to explain the point more deeply and to clarify Paul's attitude. When he states that the second group of preachers, characterized by goodwill, was acting "out of love" for him, he is not suggesting that *he* dominated their message; clearly Christ was the focus, not Paul. Rather, within the politics of the Roman church they were Paul's supporters. The emphasis on love stems from its centrality in the teachings of both Jesus and Paul. The church must be centered on love (John 13:34–35; Rom 12:9–13; Gal 5:13), and Paul was immensely encouraged by that love directed toward him.

These believers rightly understood what lay behind Paul's imprisonment, and the basis of that loving support was their realization that he had been "put here (in prison) for the defense of the gospel." "Put here" translates *keimai*, a term that means to "lie down" or "recline" but that was often used figuratively of a person who had been "set in place" or appointed to an official position. Here the implication is that they understood that God had placed Paul in confinement and had sent him to Rome to "defend the gospel." Much as John calls Jesus' destiny the "hour" of his passion (John 7:30; 8:20; 12:23, 27), so Paul refers to his chains as a divine "appointment."

Paul's major purpose was not to proclaim his own innocence or to win his release from prison but to defend the Christian faith before the chief opponents of Christian truth, the Roman hierarchy. Paul and his supporters realized that it was not Paul alone who was on trial for his life; he was defending the right of Christianity to exist in the Roman world as a religious movement, and the faith itself depended on the outcome. Paul certainly did not know what Nero would do in just five short years—declare Christianity an outlaw religion—but he could see the handwriting on the wall with the growing Roman hostility. There was an unbelievable amount at stake, and his backers recognized the pressure he was under and gave him their full support, trying to pick up the slack regarding the issues in the Roman church.

OTHERS OUT OF SELFISH AMBITION (1:17)

Notice the deliberate contrast between the two groups. Paul's supporters "knew" the situation (v. 16) and interpreted it correctly, while his opponents merely "supposed" or "assumed" that their perspective was correct (v. 17). Moreover, they were moti-vated by "selfish ambition" based on their envy of Paul's popu-larity in the church. The Greek term here (*eritheia*) refers to an ambitious, self-centered spirit that was willing to divide the group in order to further personal aspirations for power (see Phil 2:3; Jas 3:14, 16). It is virtually synonymous with "envy and rivalry" in verse 15a.

Clearly these opponents were going so far as to use their preaching of the gospel as an occasion to increase opposition to Paul—to "stir up trouble" for him. "Trouble" in this context is *thlipsis*, the basic New Testament word for "tribulation" or "affliction," indicating the difficulties and problems intrinsic to life in an evil world. Here the term probably carries several con-notations, referring not just to opposition within the church and persecution from outsiders (perhaps even from Paul's cap-tors), but also to the inner pain that all of this would bring Paul. There also may have been an aspect of the "messianic woes"—the doctrine expressed in Colossians 1:24 and Revelation 6:9–11 that the sufferings of God's people are the sufferings of Christ and the messianic community, and that the completion of the God-appointed amount of suffering would usher in the end of history.

The exact identity of these opponents is difficult to pin down. Some think this situation is related to the problems under-lying Paul's letter to the Romans, written about five years ear-lier (AD 57). There the conflict was between Jewish and Gentile Christians (Rom 14:1–15:13), and Paul told them to respect each other and quit fighting. Perhaps the opponents here (in Phil 1:17) were some Jewish Christians who were unhappy with that let-ter (Romans), but there is no evidence to support this hypothesis. The Judaizing false teachers of 3:1–4:1, below, also were a differ-ent group, present in Philippi rather than in Rome. It is possible that the preachers of 1:17 interpreted Paul's imprisonment as a sign that God was not behind him, but we cannot be sure.

We do know that envy and selfish ambition were behind their opposition. This may well have been simple jealousy over Paul's prominence in the community—the feeling that they themselves deserved the status accorded him and a desire to turn people away from him and toward themselves. This is a motivation we have all experienced and can understand, despite our recognition that we should rejoice when one of our fellow saints achieves great things for the Lord. This problem is as alive today as it was in the first century. I live an hour away from Willow Creek Community Church, a congregation of more than 20,000 on the outskirts of Chicago, and know people who pass dozens of churches to worship there. It would be easy for me as a Bible teacher to be jealous of Willow Creek's remarkable success rather than thankful for all the people this church is reaching.

The Important Consideration— Proclaiming Christ (1:18a)

The point of all this is clear: Paul regarded any opposition to be irrelevant so long as the gospel was being proclaimed. His maturity and dedication to Christ and his calling were incredible. Note the development thus far: The result both of Paul's imprisonment and of the opposition he had endured had been the advancement of the gospel. Nothing else mattered. All the negatives in Paul's life were nothing so long as the gospel was advancing by these means.

The key? "In every way, whether from false motives or true, Christ is preached." Now this does not mean that Paul enjoyed all these troubles. He was not a medieval monk chaining himself in a cave so he could be bitten by spiders or snakes. His joy was in Christ proclaimed, not in his personal afflictions. All that mattered was Christ and the spread of the gospel. If that demanded his personal suffering, it was a price he was willing to pay. Paul's remark about preaching Christ "in every way" included both his chains and his opposition. His opponents' "false motives" meant that they were using even their gospel preaching in order to hurt Paul, but his point is that despite this ulterior motive the gospel was going forth.

So, Paul concludes, "because of this, I rejoice." As long as evangelism continued he had no concern about how many people might turn against him. His joy was in the spread of the gospel, not in the number of people who applauded him. He viewed all of these impediments—his chains and his opponents—from God's perspective, that of Romans 8:28. Paul's circumstances were "working together for the best" and enhancing his true goal—that through everything he did and endured, God's name would be glorified and God's truth would be proclaimed.

———

The Philippian believers were very concerned about Paul and needed to hear the latest news regarding his imprisonment and trial. In Philippians 1:12-18a Paul provides an update and demonstrates his joy even in his adversity, for God was manifesting his sovereign will in every aspect of the situation. Paul had been thrown into two different prisons for a combined total of four years, with the direct result that the gospel was advancing in miraculous ways. Many preachers had turned against him and were trying to cause immense trouble for him, but even amid this opposition God was causing the gospel to go forth *through them*. The only response Paul could give was joy.

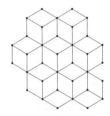

THE STATE OF PAUL AND THE
GOSPEL IN ROME—PART II

(1:18b–26)

Having shown God's control over his present crisis as a prisoner in Rome, Paul now turns to the immediate future and to news about his actual trial before Nero. What he has to say is significant in several ways. If he felt joy in the midst of his present trials, he experienced it that much more in light of God's sovereign control of the future. Nero's decision in Paul's legal case would be announced quite soon, and, either way, Paul would not be in chains much longer. Of course, he did not know whether his "deliverance" would be temporary, enabling a trip back to the Philippians, or eternal, constituting a trip to his true home in heaven. In either case Christ would be glorified, and that was all that mattered. God's (not Caesar's) decision was to be announced any day, and Paul was at peace with whatever direction the verdict might go. This paragraph is one of the greatest Christian meditations ever written on the true meaning of "leaving this life."

PAUL DISCUSSES THE POSSIBLE OUTCOMES AND THE TRUE PURPOSE—THE GLORY OF CHRIST (1:18B-20)

JOY IN HIS FUTURE DELIVERANCE (1:18B-19)

Paul begins on the same note with which he ended the previous section—joy in the Lord. However, the tone changes, for there the joy was in the present tense, with Paul rejoicing in his current circumstances. Here it is in the future tense: Paul affirms that no matter what happens God will orchestrate the events for his glory and Paul's deliverance. The future in any case would be characterized by unremitting joy; he was thrilled with either outcome because he knew his Lord was in charge. Joy and trials are indissolubly linked in Scripture, part of the catechetical (official teaching) tradition of the church. James 1:2-4 commands, "Consider it pure joy" whenever any trial comes because you know that the purpose of that trial is to test your faith and produce endurance. First Peter 1:6-7 states that we can "greatly rejoice" in difficulties because such trials re-create us as pure gold before God. Paul is part of this tradition as he reacts to the coming announcement regarding his capital trial and the question of whether his future will bring release or execution. Either way he "will continue to rejoice" because whatever God decides will be for the best (Rom 8:28).

Paul does not know which way the imperial decision will go, but there is one important fact he does know: "This will turn out for my deliverance." This confident statement comes from Job 13:16, in which Job expresses his certainty that, although his fate appeared to be doomed, God would vindicate and deliver him (see also Job 13:18). Paul uses the Greek term *sōtēria* ("salvation"), which has a double meaning here. There were two courtrooms operating, the earthly court of Caesar and the heavenly court of God. Paul might be judged guilty in Caesar's court, but his vindication and salvation were certain before the judgment seat of God. Like Job, Paul did not know whether the near future held acquittal or death, but he did know that either option would mean his deliverance into the will of God. His salvation was certain and his deliverance was imminent. He would either be delivered from his imprisonment and allowed to return to the Philippians or delivered from the earthly life and ushered into his eternal salvation in heaven. He rejoiced in either possibility.

Paul's sense of assurance was grounded in two realities: the intercessory prayers of the Philippians and the supply of the Spirit from Christ. The first led to the second, in that the Philippians' prayers were answered by the provision of the Spirit. The Greek word Paul uses here (*deēsis*) speaks of petitionary prayer, and the power of corporate prayer is often stressed in the New Testament (Matt 18:19–20; Rom 15:30–33; Eph 6:18–20; Col 4:2–3). Prayer channels the presence of God into a state of affairs, and the prayers of the church channel even more of God's presence and have the power to change things. They make a mighty difference, and Paul often asked for prayer (2 Cor 1:11; 1 Thess 5:25; 2 Thess 3:1–2), strongly believing in its effectiveness. Paul prays for the Philippians in 1:3–11, and now he asks that they pray for him.

These prayers were closely linked to the provision of the Spirit (see also Gal 3:5), called "the Spirit of Jesus Christ" here to indicate that the Son as well as the Father had sent him (see also Acts 16:7; Rom 8:9; Gal 4:6; 1 Pet 1:11). There is a question as to whether the emphasis is on the Spirit being supplied by Christ to Paul or on the Spirit supplying help to Paul. I prefer to see both aspects here. The prayers of the saints led to Christ supplying the Spirit to aid Paul and produced God's will in the situation. Notice the trinitarian thrust: The Father's will is produced by Christ sending the Spirit in answer to the petitions of God's people. The title "Spirit of Jesus Christ" means that the Spirit mediates the presence of Christ to us. The Spirit's intercession in our needs constitutes Christ's living presence.

THE TRUE GOAL—THE GLORY OF CHRIST (1:20)

Paul reflects momentarily on the fact that his trial is coming to completion and prays for the courage to face whatever God might dictate. His only desire was for Christ to be praised and the gospel to progress in this world, and he did not want to get in the way of either goal. He had no doubt whatsoever that his final deliverance would indeed take place, but he was not sure about the immediate future—whether he would live or die. His "eager expectation and hope," referring to an intense longing for a certain event to take place, was for the courage to face his possible death. He didn't mind dying, but he feared not dying well. He states this desire negatively at first ("that I will in no way be ashamed") but then positively ("so that now as always Christ will be exalted in my body").

In the Old Testament the prayer that God's people not suffer shame (Pss 25:2–3; 31:17; 119:80) but instead magnify the Lord (Pss 35:26–27; 40:15–16) is frequent. Paul knew that the Lord indeed would vindicate him, but he prayed that he would have the strength to surrender to God's will and boldly face whatever God chose to do. The Greek word translated "courage" is *parrēsia*, "with all boldness," referring to an outspoken confidence to proclaim forcefully and plainly the gospel truths as Paul faced his inquisitors of the Roman tribunal.

God had called Paul to defend the gospel (1:7) and had given him this extraordinary chance to do so before the highest court in the land, and Paul wanted to make the most of this wondrous opportunity. With the prayers of the saints behind him and the empowering provision of the Spirit within him, he planned to do so with everything he had. He had no great stake in proving his innocence; God would take care of that. His focus was on exalting his Lord. "In my body" could mean simply "in me" as a person or (more likely) refer to the fact that the trial would end in either bodily death or life—"whether by life or by death" in terms of his physical existence.

PAUL DISCUSSES THE DIFFICULT CHOICE
BEFORE HIM—LIFE OR DEATH (1:21-24)

THE OPTIONS, BOTH OF WHICH ARE DESIRABLE (1:21)

This short paragraph elaborates on the "whether by life or by death" idea in verse 20 and constitutes Paul's own meditation on this topic, undoubtedly reflecting the great amount of time he had spent thinking about the life-or-death decision to be made as the trial drew to a close. From a personal standpoint Paul preferred to be sent home to God and to his true family, the saints in heaven. When he thought strategically, however, he felt that the church still needed him. So he vacillated between the two possible outcomes.

He presents his true feelings with a pair of terse and powerful sentences, translated literally "To live, Christ. To die, gain." Each part is replete with theological depth. Paul expected to live, but the totality of life in this world, he knew, was summed up in Christ. Nothing else mattered. To understand this we must go back to his earlier self-depictions as Christ's "slave" (Phil 1:1; Rom 1:1; Titus 1:1) and "prisoner" (Eph 3:1; 4:1), meaning that he belonged to Jesus completely. Paul had been captured by Christ and had no life outside of him. The primary image in the Prison Letters (Colossians, Philemon, Ephesians, and Philippians) is that everything Paul was and did was "in Christ," depicting his union with Christ and his membership in the body of Christ, the church. Christ was the sphere of his life, and everything that had meaning or value was found for him "in Christ."

Some interpreters have understood "to live" as referring not to earthly life but to the higher realm of the new creation or new humanity of Ephesians 2:14-15. This would signify that Paul incorporated in the phrase "to live" the idea of resurrection life after death—the new life we have in Christ. But there is a simple juxtaposition here between life and death and no real evidence for a more complex understanding. "To live" is synonymous with "living in the body" in verse 22. The issue here is whether Paul would be declared innocent by Nero and continue his earthly existence or would be found guilty, resulting in his execution.

For Paul, all that had value in his earthly life was found in Christ, and the natural implication for his possible execution would be that leaving this life and entering the state of death could only be "gain," since it would mean going into the presence of Christ. The idea behind "gain" is something that brings "profit" or "advantage." Paul further explores this idea in 3:7 with a sharp contrast: All earthly benefits are to be considered loss so that we can find true gain, namely Christ and eternal reward. Here in 1:21, his point is that we get to experience Christ spiritually in this life, but truly and perfectly only after death. He further explores this gain in verse 23, defining it as "to depart and be with Christ." Paul was thinking of his death as a martyr—which comes from the Greek word *martys,* meaning "witness"—and so of his testimony to Christ via his execution. So Paul's "gain" here is not just his eternal reward but also his ultimate witness, through his death, to the saving power of Christ.

The Choices Are Enumerated (1:22–24)

To go on living means fruitful labor (1:22)

There is an A-B-A pattern here, with verses 22 and 24 detailing the possibility of Paul's release and verse 23 the possibility of his execution. Returning to the question of "fleshly" (Greek: *en sarki*) or earthly life, Paul defines it as "fruitful labor," most likely picturing his gospel preaching as the "fruit" of his hard work for Christ. The proclamation of Christ and the winning of converts together constituted the true harvest for Paul. He was planting trees in God's garden and grafting wild olive shoots on God's tree (Rom 11:17), and he was overjoyed at the prospect. This is the "gain" of verse 21—seeing the fruit of a life lived well for Christ. But for Paul the choice was between fruitful labor in earthly life and being with Christ for eternity.

There is incredible value in both, so he exclaims, "Yet what shall I choose?" This does not mean that Paul believed he could somehow control God and select the outcome; rather, it expresses his conflicting thoughts as to his preference. A better paraphrase is "Which do I prefer?" Paul "does not know" which outcome is best; he simply could not choose between such incredibly momentous alternatives. One held advantages for the church, the other for Paul himself. The next two verses will explore the options and explain why both would constitute desirable gains.

To depart and be with Christ is far better (1:23)

Paul states that he was "torn between the two" possibilities, with the Greek verb (synechō) meaning that he was "dominated" or "completely controlled" by the dilemma. His conflicting emotions had totally gripped him, and how could it have been otherwise?

Paul's most powerful personal desire by far was "to depart and be with Christ." Most of us would make this kind of decision on the basis of our current physical situation. If we are young and healthy we have little desire to leave this life. I myself am older (seventy-three as I write this commentary), and my basic belief is that "my body hates me"—so I long for my resurrection body. Paul was not thinking this way. His concern was not for health but "to be with Christ," and his death or "departure" would simply be the means by which his ultimate gain would be realized.

Elsewhere in his writings, Paul describes two stages of life after death. First, in 2 Corinthians 5:1-10, Paul says that when our "earthly tent" is dissolved we immediately begin an intermediate state in which our spirit is "away from our body and at home with the Lord" (2 Cor 5:8). Then in 1 Corinthians 15:51-54 and 1 Thessalonians 4:13-18, Paul explains the second stage: When Christ returns, our spirit will be joined to our new resurrection body and our final eternal state will commence. Here in Philippians, Paul is thinking especially about being "with Christ," starting in the first stage and continuing in the second. His point is that this outcome is "better by far," for entering eternal life is so much more profitable for us personally than remaining in a temporary, finite existence.

To remain is better for the Philippians (1:24)

The first alternative would be better personally for Paul, but the second would be preferable corporately for the Philippian church. There is a huge difference between "desire" and "necessity," and corporate need had to take a far greater priority for Paul than personal longing. Paul recognized that "to remain in the body," to continue his earthly existence and ministry, was "more necessary" for the Philippian believers. Their situation outweighed his own desires, so he expected God to spare him for further ministry on earth. Paul's servant heart and maturity as he placed their good above his own provides a model for all of us.

The Joyous Expectation—Paul Would Remain with Them (1:25-26)

Paul now draws his conclusion. Regarding Nero as little more than a tool of God, Paul's entire focus was on the true Sovereign Lord who would either take him to his true home in heaven or send him back to the Philippians and the other congregations. Paul's language here is quite strong. He is "convinced," but not by the legal arguments made in Roman courts over the last four years. It is the logic of divine mission that drives the future, so he does not "think" he "might" be freed but "knows" he "will" be freed.

Some have called this sudden certainty the result of "prophetic inspiration." To an extent that is close to the case, though Paul does not employ prophetic language here. Rather, he is relating to the Philippians the process God has led him through in his own developing understanding. The uncertainty behind verses 22-24 reflects the lengthy period during which Paul had gone back and forth on his preference, while verses 25-26 confidently express a recent conclusion God had led him to discover. The issues at Philippi that become evident later in the letter needed a mature hand, and God had made known to Paul that he was the one God had chosen for the task. Therefore, Paul was convinced he would be set free to perform the "fruitful labor" (v. 22) in Philippi that God had for him.

The purpose of Paul's "remaining" with the Philippians was their "progress and joy in the faith." There were three major problems facing the church in Philippi: persecution (1:27–30), dissension (2:1–18; 4:2–3), and false teaching (3:1–4:1). Paul felt a deep and abiding joy due to his close and loving relationships with these people, but his and their joy was being threatened by these problems (he writes "with tears," 3:18). They needed to advance in Christian maturity and win the victory over those things to find the joy that should have been theirs.

The Greek text of verse 25 could be describing "joyous progress" or "greater and greater joy," but Paul most likely is referring to separate but related items (both "progress" and "joy," as in the NIV). Paul knew the Philippians needed him because their problems were hindering their growth in the Lord. Note that "progress/advance" language frames this section; the central issue is the advancement of the Christian faith among both unbelievers ("advance the gospel," v. 12) and believers ("your progress," v. 25). The cause of Christ was being hindered by the inability of this church to solve these problems, and they needed Paul's guidance to do so.

As they advanced "in the faith" and found victory in all three of these problem areas, their joy would increase exponentially. One cannot progress in the faith without progressing also in that joy that faith brings. Most likely the "joy" indicated here is both **eschatological** joy in the Spirit, in light of the living hope that is ours, as well as a general happiness based on knowing that God is on our side, guiding and empowering us as we face life's challenges.

If verse 25 is the immediate goal for the Philippian church, verse 26 is the long-range goal. When they have progressed in the faith and regained their joy in the Lord, Paul declares, the believers' "boasting in Christ Jesus will abound on account of me." The word "abound" in this context (as in verse 9) means to increase or overflow in the church. The Greek phrase here is interesting, reading literally "your boasting might increase in Christ Jesus in me." This increase comes in three levels: Their joy and their boasting begin in Christ Jesus, then proceed to Paul (whose ministry is the channel through whom Christ works), and finally overflow into the church itself.

This kind of "boasting" is obviously positive rather than negative; it means to "exult" or "glory" in something and tell others how great it is. The idea is that when the Philippians have conquered their problems and rediscovered their joy in Christ, their exultation in everything Christ has done will overflow. As we experience the Lord's work in our lives, we are inspired to glory in him—and that glory abounds more and more, becoming a flood of joy and praise that uplifts everyone around us.

There is a difference of opinion as to the thrust of the Greek phrase *en emoi*. Some English translations render this "because of me" or something similar (NIV, ESV, HCSB, LEB, NET) and see Paul's ministry as the reason for the change among the Philippians. Other translations have "in me," regarding Paul as the object of their pride ("boast in me," NASB, KJV). The first approach is probably better, but this leads to another question: Is the reason for the change Paul's reunion with the Philippians (evoking encouragement in a general sense) or his work among them (helping them solve their difficulties after he is released)? The larger context of verses 20–26 makes the latter option more likely. Paul believed the Lord would enable his return to Philippi so he could help the believers overcome their challenges and rediscover their joy in the Lord. On this basis their exultation would overflow.

———

Philippians 1:18b–26 is a valuable meditation on the true meaning of death for Christians. God has given us a will to live—to remain among family and loved ones and to serve God as long as possible. In Paul's conflicting thoughts in this passage, we see ourselves. It is critical for us to come to grips with what our death truly means. It is "the last enemy to be destroyed" (1 Cor 15:26), but it also constitutes a transition onward to eternal life and joy in heaven. We will be with God forever, and all sorrow and hardship will be over (Rev 21:3–4). Both perspectives are essential for the saints as each of us faces our own death and departure to the Lord's side.

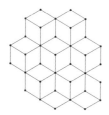

DEALING WITH PERSECUTION AND DISSENSION
(1:27–2:4)

Having completed the news about his circumstances, Paul now addresses the needs of the Philippians, beginning with the persecution and suffering they were experiencing (1:27-30) and then turning to the importance of Christian unity and humility (2:1-18). The gospel is central to both sections and draws them together. The Philippians were "partners in the gospel" with Paul (1:5). All of his experiences, including his chains, had served to advance the gospel (v. 12). Now Paul exhorts them that in all they are going through they should conduct themselves in a way "worthy of the gospel" (v. 27). The core of this passage is ethical exhortation. Paul presses the Philippian believers to live the Christian life to the full and to make certain that in all their difficulties they are living like Christ and working together in unity.

PAUL CALLS FOR STEADFASTNESS AND UNITY IN THE MIDST OF PERSECUTION (1:27-30)

THE PROPER CONDUCT—WORTHY OF THE GOSPEL (1:27-28)

The NIV's "whatever happens" is actually the Greek adverb *monon*, meaning "the one and only thing" that Paul wished to discuss. Paul was placing all the problems of the Philippians, as well as their solutions, under a single comprehensive category: "Walk worthily of the gospel." Everything was related to the gospel of Christ, and the answer for each problem was related to the Philippians' Christian walk. It is notable that in verse 27 Paul does not use *peripateō*, the Greek verb commonly used in the sense of "live (or walk) as a Christian." Instead, he chooses *politeuomai*, a verb with the political overtones of "live properly as a citizen"—which would have made a great deal of sense in a Roman fortress city like Philippi. This is connected to Philippians 3:20 and the theological truth that believers are citizens of heaven, strangers to this world (1 Pet 1:2, 17; 2:11). Accordingly, Paul's instruction to the believers is rightly translated "live as citizens of heaven" (Phil 1:27 NLT)

Paul is combining both identities—"citizens of heaven" and "strangers to this world." Jesus does something similar in Matthew 17:25–27, where he teaches the disciples they are both children of the kingdom (and so exempt from paying taxes) as well as residents of the earthly kingdom (so obliged to pay taxes nonetheless). Believers are doubly responsible to be model citizens because they belong first to God's kingdom and therefore are to be strictly faithful to their earthly duties as well. This is echoed in 1 Peter 2:12, where the saints are told to maintain a lifestyle of absolute goodness, so that their opponents will be convicted by the saints' impeccable lives, be converted, and glorify God. Faithful Christian living enhances the power of the gospel.

STEADFAST, UNITED, AND FEARLESS (1:27–28A)

The first part of this sentence builds on the two options of verses 22–24. Paul expresses that he will "come and see you" if he is freed and "remains in the body," or will "hear about you" if he is not acquitted and awaits execution. As stated in verses 25–26 he believed that he would be freed and planned to visit the Philippians as soon as that transpired. He could not, however, be sure of the outcome of the trial, and the problems facing him were quite severe. In light of his situation he would be sending Timothy in the near future and would hear from him, hoping to be "cheered" by good news (2:19). Either way, he anticipated that the Philippians would "stand firm in the one Spirit." There were four areas in which Paul wanted these Christians to progress spiritually, as summarized by four descriptions:

1. Steadfast—standing firm for Christ in the midst of struggle and severe persecution. As Paul goes on to say in 1:28-30, the Philippian believers, considering the opposition and suffering they were enduring, were in danger of being overwhelmed by fear. So he asks them to remain strong and secure in the midst of hardship. This is a military metaphor depicting a soldier remaining firm in the midst of battle. It is similar to the armor of God passage in Ephesians 6:10-13, written just a few months earlier, where Paul exhorted the saints to "take your stand against the devil's schemes ... to stand your ground, and after you have done everything, to stand." In the struggle against the evil powers, demonic or Roman, it was essential to remain steadfast and strong in the Lord.

2. United—working together as one and strengthening each other in the midst of adversity. There is some debate as to whether "the one Spirit" should be understood as the Holy Spirit (NIV) or the human spirit (KJV, NRSV, ESV, NLT, HCSB, LEB, LASB, and NET). If the Holy Spirit, this would parallel Ephesians 4:4, where Paul emphasized "one body and one Spirit" (see also 1 Cor 12:13; Eph 2:18) to stress the importance of unity in the church, as well as Philippians 4:1, where Paul commands the believers to "stand firm in the Lord." However, many interpreters prefer to read 1:27 with a stress on the unity of the "spirit" of the church, translating the phrase as "stand firm with one purpose." This is a difficult determination, for both renderings make sense of the passage. I believe that a focus on the Holy Spirit is

the slightly superior option, as Paul anchors the Philippians' strength to remain firm in the empowering presence of the Spirit, and the unity of the Godhead becomes the basis for the unity of the church. There is both a vertical (the Triune Godhead) and a horizontal (the one body of Christ) basis for the united power of God's people as they take their stand against evil.

3. Striving together—like soldiers fighting side by side against a common foe. This was the real basis for the invincible nature of the Roman army. Each battalion (called a "century") would fight in a square, with the soldiers beside and behind one another, forming a single, nearly impregnable unit. The chaotic barbarian armies facing such a disciplined onslaught never had a chance. Paul pictures the saints standing side by side in the same way, strengthening and helping one another[1] as they faced Roman aggression against them. Disunity among believers, as we will see in 2:1–18 and 4:2–3, is very dangerous and nearly always presages spiritual defeat. The one Spirit works to preserve the one church, and the truth is that we desperately need one another as we contend for "the faith of the gospel," referring to the Christian faith that stems from the gospel of Christ. The task of God's people is to take the gospel to the world, and to do so we must have a united faith that strengthens us to fulfill that calling.

4. Fearless—refusing to allow the realm of darkness to intimidate them (v. 28a). This further defines "standing firm," pointing to the absence of fear in the face of relentless hostility. To be steadfast is to ignore the intimidation factor. The roar of a lion or a bear is intended to paralyze

---

1. The literal statement is "striving with one soul" (*mia psychē*), referring to the unity of purpose that is to typify God's people. It is this second phrase, not "the one Spirit," that carries the idea of the united "purpose" of the saints.

its potential prey. It is said that the most effective response to a menacing bear is to look the animal in the eye and roar back, for bears slink away in the face of fearless defiance. The Greek word Paul uses here for "frightened" (*ptyromenoi*) suggests horses stampeding on the battlefield and throwing their riders in terror. The followers of Christ refuse to be petrified or to run off in fright; they respond to their opponents by the one Spirit and as the one people of God, armed with the invincible power of gospel truth. We remember the words of Jesus in Matthew 10:28: "Do not be afraid of those who kill the body but cannot kill the soul." After all, as Paul has just pointed out in verse 21, for the believer "to die is gain."

While some have speculated that the opponents Paul mentions in verse 28a were the Judaizers of 3:1–4:1, such a connection is unlikely. The Judaizers posed a threat from within the Christian movement, but the adversaries of 1:28 were outsiders—Romans who rejected Christianity and persecuted God's people.

The Two Signs—Destruction and Salvation (1:28b)

There are grammatical difficulties in verse 28b, which reads in the NIV, "This is a sign to them that they will be destroyed, but that you will be saved." "This" is actually translating the Greek pronoun *hētis* ("which"), referring to the commands of verses 27–28a to walk worthily by standing firm and fearless for the gospel. The meaning of the twofold sign is difficult to ascertain. The Greek term translated "to them" (NIV) also can be understood as "with reference to them," meaning that the sign was evident to the believers rather than to their opponents. It is the Philippian Christians who recognize the two destinies— the unbelievers' destruction and their own salvation.[2] Another

---

2. Several interpreters think this is still a sign to unbelievers, even though they do not perceive it as such.

possibility is that Paul is referring to both groups: The unbelievers interpreted the persecution as a sign of the Christians' destruction, while the believers perceived it as signifying their salvation. This view, though interesting, seems a little too complex for the wording.

It is probably best to take a third approach and recognize a more direct thrust in Paul's statement: The sign and its message are part of the gospel and are intended for both groups. Those unbelievers who were open to the gospel were becoming aware that their persecution of God's people would indeed bring destruction upon themselves and that the saints would ultimately find eternal salvation. The difference has to do with whether they recognized the central truth that both outcomes— destruction and salvation—would be accomplished *by God*. As soon as one sees the hand of God behind the process, everything becomes clear. Those who rejected God would never understand, but the sign was still meant for them and was intended to wake them up to the truth. This would be accomplished as the persecutors witnessed the unity and strength by which those they are seeking to intimidate endured the painful process of persecution (as in 1 Pet 2:12).

THE GIFT OF SUFFERING (1:29–30)

The goal of suffering—for Paul (1:29)

Salvation does not mean a cessation of suffering but points rather to a triumph over suffering. After discussing the final deliverance, the salvation that is the God-given destiny for his people, Paul says, "It has been granted to you on behalf of Christ not only to believe on him, but also to suffer for him." Suffering is presented here not as a tragic event but as a grace-gift from God. Since the Christian life is a sharing of the life of Christ by each believer, the experience must include participation in his suffering. This will be explored further in 3:10, where "the fellowship of his sufferings" is seen as part of "knowing him."

The early church's dogma included what has been called "the messianic woes"—the idea that the messianic community would share in the life of the Suffering Servant-Messiah (Isa 52–53). According to this teaching (described in Jewish writings like 1 Enoch 47:1–4; 4 Ezra 4:35–37), God had allotted a certain amount of suffering for the Messiah and his people, and when that destined amount was reached, the end would come. These afflictions would constitute the "birth pangs" of the end of history (Dan 12:1; Mark 3:20; Rom 8:22; 2 Thess 2:11–12; Rev 6:9; 13:7; see also 4 Ezra 13:16–19). The sufferings of God's people are part of their messianic call and part of what it means to be "in Christ." This involves not general suffering, like illness or economic woes, but a specific kind of suffering "for him" or "on behalf of him"—public humiliation, slander, and other forms.

Paul's point in Philippians 1:29 is that believing in Christ produces suffering on behalf of Christ. Jesus provides the classic statement on this in John 15:18–25, where he gives a syllogistic proof:

> The world hates Jesus.
> Jesus loves and abides in his disciples (they are one).
> Therefore, the world hates his disciples.

Christianity is not just another religion. It is exclusive—the *only* path to God and eternal life. As Jesus also said in John 3:19–20, darkness hates light because the light of Christ exposes its pretense to be light for the lie that it is. We live in a culture where, fortunately, there is not a great deal of religious persecution, and Paul is not saying that we should look for it. But we must at all times be ready to suffer for Christ and count it a privilege when such trials come.

The model for the struggle—Paul (1:30)

Paul wanted the Philippian believers to know that they were not alone, nor were they the first to pass through that deep valley of affliction. Theirs was, in Paul's words, "the same struggle you saw I had." The Greek term translated "struggle" is *agōn*, which depicts an athletic contest that demands strength and endurance. For Paul, the believers' conflict had eternal consequences and was being fought not just against pagans (in this case Romans) but also against the cosmic powers of darkness: "For our struggle is not against flesh and blood, but against ... the powers of this dark world" (Eph 6:12). At stake is the spiritual state of the church and also the spread of the gospel to the very forces arrayed against believers. There are three levels in view: the individual struggle, the corporate battles of the church, and the external movement of God's salvation to the unsaved. Paul's battle took place in the very public arena of the imperial court, while that of his readers was occurring in the homes and workplaces of Philippi. But it was essentially "the same struggle"—the work of God versus the evil powers.

The believers at Philippi first "saw" Paul's suffering when he founded the church there on his second missionary journey, during a visit when he was beaten and thrown into prison (Acts 16:19–40). They watched firsthand his unflagging endurance and incredible model for relying on God while enduring great hardship. Picture Paul and Silas, after having been scourged and chained to the walls of their filthy prison, praying and singing hymns while waiting for God to act. What an example of faith in action!

Now the Philippians "hear" of Paul in his more serious and lengthy imprisonment. His faith and endurance—as well as his central concern for the spread of the gospel over his personal welfare—continue unabated, as in his earlier struggle. Paul's point in Philippians 1:30 is that he identifies with the believers' difficult situation and knows exactly what they are going through. It was Paul's hope that these Christians would emulate his trust in God and "wait upon the Lord" (Isa 40:31) as they passed through this suffering on behalf of Christ. Understanding how few afflictions we have experienced for Christ, we must not let ourselves become discouraged by our paltry problems.[3] Instead, we must look to the same Lord Paul did and trust him to alleviate our faltering spirits.

PAUL CALLS FOR HUMILITY IN THE MIDST OF DISSENSION (2:1-4)

FOUR CHRISTIAN EXPERIENCES (2:1)

The sentence begins with "Therefore," showing that verses 1-4 are building on the preceding section. To conduct themselves worthily of the gospel (1:27) the Philippians must resolve any ongoing conflicts in their church and demonstrate unity in Christ. The exhortation is based in four spiritual realities these people had experienced as a result of being children of God and members of Christ's body. Paul uses a conditional ("if") sentence that portrays these spiritual realities as givens; the four occurrences of "if" can almost be translated "since." In light of these divine gifts, Paul is saying, the Philippians should act differently from the rest of the world, which is driven by status-seeking and rivalry. If they have actually experienced these things (and they have), there are certain areas of their behavior that must change. However, these believers did not seem to have fully given themselves to the way of Christ—which is marked by humility, as Paul would soon explain—so the "if" statements exhort them to get busy overcoming their difficulties. They have experienced all these blessings, but they are not acting like it. The basis for Paul's appeal is fourfold.

---

3. We might find ourselves in the pits when we cannot afford to sell our 1,500-square-foot home and buy a 2,200-square-foot home, or when we have the flu for over a week and can't seem to get rid of it. We cannot begin to understand what Paul and the early Christians were going through!

1. "Encouragement from Being United with Christ" (literally, "in Christ")

There are three aspects to the range of meaning in the Greek term *paraklēsis*, from exhortation to encouragement to comfort. One could almost say that the three build on each other, as exhortation produces encouragement, which in turn leads to comfort. The latter two nuances of meaning apply to this context. There is a tendency among recent interpreters to prefer "comfort" or "consolation" in light of the context of suffering. This would be akin to 2 Corinthians 1:5: "For just as we share abundantly in the sufferings of Christ, so also our comfort abounds through Christ."

In many ways all three aspects are part of what Paul is saying here, and each of the three has been argued by scholars as his thrust. The exhortations of the church and of Paul in this letter were helping these believers find encouragement in Christ, and that was providing comfort in the midst of their tribulations. However, in this instance I believe encouragement is the nuance Paul intends, for the comfort that results is the secondary spiritual reality that will come next. The Philippians' union with Christ provided encouragement, and the love of Christ produced comfort. They had been experiencing these wonderful facets of their walk with Christ, and if they heeded Paul those blessings would continue as they learned to live in unity.

2. "Comfort from His Love" (literally, "from love")

Paul now portrays the consolation or solace derived from Christ's encouraging presence. This second term, *paramythion*, is a near synonym to *paraklēsis*, having the same three connotations (exhortation, encouragement, and comfort), and it likely was intended by Paul to build on the first. Still, the thrust is similar, suggesting a challenge or exhortation that encourages and produces comfort. The first spiritual reality centers on encouraging, and the second details the result—comforting. Christ's presence encourages, and love comforts.

The primary question is whose love is meant—Christ's, Paul's, or the church's? I agree with those who see all three sources at work here. It would appear that Paul deliberately avoided using a qualifying term, intending this to be construed in the broadest possible way. Christ's love was the basis, and out of his love stemmed the believers' experience of Paul's love, as well as of their love for each other. The point here is that the church's experience of love, on all three levels, was being threatened by dissension and false teaching.

Paul describes the significance of comfort in 2 Corinthians 1:3-4, where he speaks of "the God of all comfort, who comforts us in all our troubles, so that we can comfort those in any trouble with the comfort we ourselves receive from God." Comfort is a major ministry for the church, and we need to realize that the very trials we encounter become part of our later ministry as we use the process of our own recovery to comfort and help those who are going through similar difficulties.

3. "Common Sharing in the Spirit" (literally, "fellowship of the Spirit")

There is unanimous support for the view that Paul is referencing the Holy Spirit rather than the human spirit, but the implication of koinōnia in this context is more problematic. This Greek term connotes partnership and sharing, as in 1:5, when Paul spoke of the believers' "partnership in the gospel." In Philippians 3:10 he will talk about the "fellowship of [Christ's] suffering"—of participation in the messianic suffering of Christ.

Here in 2:1 the exact thrust is difficult to ascertain. Did Paul have in view believers' fellowship with the Holy Spirit or their fellowship within the church made possible by the Spirit? Is the Spirit the subject, providing the sharing, or is he the object, receiving our fellowship? Once again, these options are not mutually exclusive. Paul is stressing our sharing in the Spirit, but it is a *common* sharing (as the NIV indicates); we are heirs together of the Spirit (Eph 1:13, 14; 4:30) and thereby share the Spirit with each other. The result of our sharing with one another is a Spirit-fellowship in which the Spirit dwells within us and enables us to overcome our differences and experience a common bond in Christ. This is the answer to the problem of dissension that underlies this section of Philippians. The Spirit brings us together in oneness and removes the very basis for conflicts and power struggles among us.

4. "Tenderness and Compassion"

The Greek terms (*splanchna kai oiktirmos*) look to the body's inner parts, particularly the intestines, which were thought to contain the emotions of a person (hence the KJV's "bowels and mercies"). Once again, by not adding "of God" or "of Christ," Paul suggests a general experience of tenderness and compassion. Still, it seems likely that he was thinking primarily of divine sympathy, as in the many Old Testament passages that speak of God's mercy and compassion (for example, Neh 9:19, 28; Pss 24:6; 145:9). Paul's first three "if" statements in Philippians 2:1 center on the actions of the Triune Godhead, and it is probable that this last one does as well. As before, the church's experience of divine blessing also is connoted. Christ's compassion sustains the cares and mercies of the church for its members.

Once again, this spiritual reality offered an antidote for the dissension that was threatening the Philippian church. If God's tender love that had consoled the believers in the past were to continue into the future, any conflicts that might disable the church would be replaced by congregational care. When we are busy showing tender love to people, we can hardly at the same time be working against them.

FOUR NEEDED INTERNAL QUALITIES (2:2)

Verse 1 included four "if" clauses, and this verse contains the conclusion, the "then" clause. Paul is saying, essentially, "If you have experienced these things, then you should make my joy complete." As we have noted more than once, Paul was particularly close to the Philippian believers because they kept in constant contact with him and supported him strongly (4:10–18). So he felt joy whenever he thought of them (1:3–4; 4:1). His tactful challenge to them here is that his joyous relationship with them was nonetheless somehow incomplete, and that it would reach fullness if they avoided troublesome conflicts in their church. It is clear that the admonition here was the result of love; all that Paul says is heartfelt. The four spiritual qualities here parallel the four spiritual experiences of verse 1 and form a **chiasm** for emphasis:

> A like-minded
>> B the same love
>> B′ one in spirit
> A′ one mind

The first spiritual quality the Philippians need is like-mindedness; a literal translation of the Greek text is "thinking the same thing" (stated again in 2:5: "the same mindset as Christ Jesus"). Paul's reference is to a person who thinks a certain way, as in those who "think differently" in 3:15 or those with earthly-centered minds in 3:19. The call here in 2:2 is for every member of the church to set aside any quarrels and center their minds on Christ. Certainly this does not mean they have had to agree on everything or become carbon copies of one another. Rather, they were to have the same mindset regarding the essentials, primarily the things of Christ.

Paul does not convey any specifics about the strife in the Philippian church, beyond his reference to the personal conflict between Euodia and Syntyche (4:2–3). The dispute between these women, who were leaders of some kind, could have been the sole source of contention, or this may have been one situation among many. We do not know the precise cause, but we do know the apparent result—dissension and fractured relationships. Whatever was happening at Philippi, the issue Paul addresses is the mental disposition of the congregation. Brothers and sisters in Christ should not be at cross-purposes from each other; they need to unite in Christ and with each other in their thinking.

The second need is to recover "the same love," building on 1:9, where Paul prayed that their "love may abound more and more." This overflowing love should produce unity of purpose, because love has a servant's heart and continually gives, as Paul will state in the next two verses. When we have experienced the sacrificial love of Christ (seen in vv. 6–8, below) and have the same love toward one another, self-centeredness disappears, and there is no longer a basis for infighting in the community.

The first two qualities result in the third, "being one in spirit." This concept is expressed in Greek with a single word, *sympsychoi*, which means to experience harmony, to be united in spirit, to be "soul brothers." Consequently, it points not to the Holy Spirit but to the human spirit. This spiritual oneness removes any discord or conflict within the church. When we are united with Christ, who "made himself nothing" (v. 7), we can hardly feel ourselves superior to others. The unity achieved will enable people to work together as one rather than quarrel over petty issues.

The final quality, being "of one mind" or "thinking the one thing," essentially repeats the first. This clearly is Paul's major point—calling for a unity of purpose in Christ, with the believers moving together in the same direction as they follow him. When we each take our own path, chaos and conflict characterize the church. But when our minds come together and follow the gospel with the same set of goals, peace and harmony flow.

The Primary Need for Humility (2:3–4)

In order to live as soul-brothers-and-sisters who were like-minded in Christ, the Philippians needed to adopt certain attitudes and do certain things; these are spelled out in the next two verses. Conflict is almost always the result of self-seeking motives and behaviors, and Paul's commands here are about pursuing the opposite course.

To begin with, these believers should "do nothing out of selfish ambition or vain conceit." Both of these attitudes stem from a self-centered mindset. The first was used back in 1:17 to describe the egocentric preachers who opposed Paul; here, as there, it depicts a person willing to divide the group over a selfish personal agenda. I have known a few narcissistic preachers in my day, and they always ended up splitting their churches. Such people look at their colleagues as rivals and constantly try to undermine them. Always looking out for "number one," their goal is never to help the people around them, but to use others to gain greater power for themselves.

"Vain conceit" is the flipside of "selfish ambition." The Greek term, *kenodoxia*, describes a worthless or empty desire for glory—a mindset that cares only to enhance an inflated view of self. Such vanity is self-promoting and ends up with a meaningless self-glorification that ends up helping no one and accomplishing nothing beyond satisfying the ego. Such people often become famous and quite wealthy, but when their lives are examined closely, no one but themselves have emerged better off through their efforts. We have all met people like this—attention-seekers who cannot get enough of the limelight and who are willing to ride roughshod over anyone who threatens to get in their way. Nothing good ever comes from such a motivation.

The two sinful qualities in Philippians 2:3a define the mentality of the world. In contrast, Paul now turns to the proper Christian mindset as defined by "humility." The Greek word he uses is *tapeinophrosynē*, a compound word literally meaning "lowly mind" and describing a person who considers herself a servant of those around her. In verses 3b-4, Paul gives what I consider to be the single best definition of humility I have read anywhere. There are two parts of this biblical understanding of the "lowly servant" mindset. First, in humility you "value others above yourselves" (v. 3; compare Rom 12:3). This means that when you interact with others you consider them more important and seek to serve them rather than use them to your own ends. The mind refuses to dwell inwardly on its own desires but forces itself to think outwardly. This selfless attitude defines Christ in Philippians 2:6–8: He refused to demand equality with God but instead "made himself nothing" and became the "slave" of all people in order to bring them to God. To value others above yourself does not mean to look down on yourself but rather means to look up to those around you, not to hate yourself but to love and serve others even more. You do not reject yourself but place your brothers and sisters on a pedestal above yourself.

The second part of the definition clarifies the first. In valuing others more than yourself, you look not "to your own interests but each of you to the interests of the others" (v. 4). The Greek verb for "look" is skopeō ("pay attention"); Paul is telling his readers to pay little heed to their own situations but to focus entirely on the people around them. Obviously, this is not intended in an absolute sense, for we do want to take care of ourselves and our families. Paul means that we are to focus on helping others more than on helping ourselves; the people around us are to get the lion's share of our attention. Interestingly, the Greek text refers literally to "the things" of others, broadening the scope to every area of life (not just "interests"). Our focus is to be on people's needs and on the whole situation in which they find themselves. Elsewhere Paul says that love is never self-seeking (1 Cor 13:5) but always aims to help others (1 Cor 10:24). That is the connotation here as well.

———

This wonderful passage introduces two problem areas in the Philippian church—the external issue of persecution and the internal matter of dissension. In both, the solution Paul recommends to his readers is simple and yet difficult to accomplish: They must change their mindset to reflect the mind of Christ. When the world turns against us, we too must take this hostility as a new depth of sharing with Christ, a reliving of his rejection by the world. We also need a new depth of union with each other, as we strengthen and encourage one another in the midst of such afflictions (as in Heb 12:12–13). When we encounter internal conflict and friends within the church turn against us, we are called to love them and to invite a change in their self-centered mindsets by demonstrating the mind of Christ. Rather than promoting the primacy of self, we all need to exemplify servant hearts and make the primacy of others the central focus of our churches. When all within the congregation focus entirely on each other's needs and desires, there will be no room for glory-seeking among God's people.

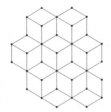

CHRIST JESUS, THE MODEL
FOR HUMILITY
(2:5–11)

We are in a section dealing with dissension and conflict in the Philippian church, and Paul has just spoken of the issues of selfish ambition and vain conceit and then defined Christian humility as the antidote. The problem was that these believers were following the ways of the world when they should have been patterning themselves after Christ. This is precisely the theme of the section that follows (vv. 5–11): Christ as the paradigm for servanthood and humility. For Paul, to be in Christ was to live like Christ (Eph 4:13, 15–16), so he quotes an early Christ-hymn on the incarnation in order to demonstrate for the Philippian believers what true humility looks like. (We will assess the passage's literary form below, in the introduction to 2:6–11.)

There has been significant discussion as to whether this passage was primarily meant to be an example of humility or a dogmatic treatise on the results of the incarnation, called by many a "drama of salvation."[1] The two are not mutually exclusive. Certainly

---

1. See especially Ralph P. Martin, "A Hymn of Christ: Philippians 2:5–11" in *Recent Interpretation and in the Setting of Early Christian Worship* (Downers Grove, IL: InterVarsity Press, 1997).

the hymn was originally written as a creedal statement on the meaning of the incarnation, yet here Paul is using it as a paradigm of humility. The theme is significant: "Like Jesus, seek humility and leave the glory up to God." The hymn functions in both ways. I have often preached it in conjunction with John 1:1–18 as a two-part message on the true meaning of Christmas. Yet in the context of the letter to the Philippians, Paul wanted his readers to see Christ as a model for their own humility (expanding on 2:3–4).

PAUL EXHORTS THE CHURCH TO EMULATE THE MINDSET OF CHRIST (2:5)

When the larger context is taken into consideration, it seems quite clear that Paul is using verse 5 quite carefully to build a bridge between the issues facing the church in verses 1–4 and the solution portrayed by Christ in verses 6–11. Two of the four spiritual qualities of verse 2 center on the mindset of the believers, calling for unity in their mental outlook. The problem is that there is no verb in the second clause; the Greek text reads literally, "Think this among you which _____ in Christ Jesus." Normally one just inserts the verb "was" (as in the first option below), but other possibilities have been suggested. Scholars have variously translated the sentence as follows, in accordance with their views of the hymn as a whole:

1. The paradigmatic view—Christ's mindset is the model we follow in our relationships, so: "which mind *was* in Christ Jesus."

2. The mystical view—The mystical union between Christ and the believer is the key to relationships, so: "Let your attitude toward one another *arise out of your life* in Christ."

3. The **ecclesiological**[2] view—The phrase "in Christ" is a creedal formula stressing membership in his body as the

---

2. "Ecclesiological" refers to the doctrine of the church; "soteriological" (on next page) refers to salvation. See the glossary for expanded definitions.

basis for church relationships, so: "Let this mind be *what is proper to have as those who are* 'in Christ.'"

4. The "drama of salvation" view—This **soteriological** approach stresses conversion as the moment when believers were inserted "in Christ," so: "Let this mind be in you which *was made possible when you were made to be* in Christ."

The context strongly favors option 1, the paradigmatic view. The dissenters were characterized by a sinful, self-centered viewpoint and needed the mindset of Christ. The emphasis here is not on "in Christ" or the moment of conversion, but on Christ's humility as the model for all believers and as the antidote to the problem of selfish ambition. When each of us has the mindset of Christ, we can finally become like-minded. The Greek is literally, "Let this mind be in you," with "in you" having a corporate thrust of the church as a whole, fitting the NIV's paraphrase "in your relationships with one another."

So this is an imperative statement, commanding that all interpersonal relationships be dominated by Christlike thinking. Throughout this challenge verses 2-4 are in mind. There can be no humility until Christ's thought-life permeates and guides our every thought. This idea connotes a strong ethical quality, demanding that our relationships with others among God's people reflect Christ at every point. He is indeed the archetypal model for the kind of mindset that produces oneness and makes relationships possible. The phrase "in Christ" means that his mindset must become the *sphere* within which our thought processes are governed. Only then can we attain the "humble-mindedness" of verse 3.

PAUL PRESENTS THE INCARNATION AS THE PARADIGM FOR HUMILITY (2:6-11)

The first question is whether verses 6-11 are a hymn or high prose. The consensus of late has been to regard the passage as an early Christian hymn developed for worship and teaching. Many hymns, like Colossians 1:15–20, are **christological**, and Philippians 2:6–11 fits well into that milieu. Still, a significant number of interpreters have strong doubts, believing instead that Paul wrote this passage as high prose (with a poetic flair).

The passage bears many criteria that favor a hymn: the introductory pronoun *hos* ("who") in verse 5; the rhythm and stately feel of the lines; the strophic pattern (see below); the use of parallel participles; the number of terms that vary from Paul's normal language; and especially the contextual dislocation of the passage. All of these characteristics, taken together, go far beyond the needs of Paul's point about humility. While it remains possible that Paul penned this section himself, it more likely is older material that was inserted here by Paul to demonstrate the mindset of Christ as a model for his followers.

The Greek text follows a three-line pattern of six strophes, or units. To demonstrate this strophic pattern, let me attempt a loose translation following the order of the Greek text:

Strophe 1	Who being in the form of God,
	He did not feel he had to seize for himself
	Equality with God
Strophe 2	But he emptied himself
	Taking on the form of a slave
	Being made in the likeness of humankind
Strophe 3	And being found in appearance as a man
	He humbled himself,
	Becoming obedient to death, even death on
	a cross.
Strophe 4	Therefore God highly exalted him
	And gave him that name
	Which is above every name.

Strophe 5   So that at the name of Jesus
              Every knee should bow
              In heaven and on earth and under
              the earth

Strophe 6   And every tongue confess
              That Jesus Christ is Lord
              To the glory of God the Father.

If this structure is correct, there are six strophes of three lines each, and Paul has expanded the third strophe to emphasize that Christ's death was on the cross, the ultimate form of humiliation. So my tentative conclusion is that this was an early creedal hymn on the meaning of the incarnation and that Paul adapted it to show Christ as the model for the needed humility of the church.[3]

CHRIST'S STATE OF HUMILIATION (2:6–8)

Christ's state of mind—refused the glory (2:6)

The hymn begins with Jesus' pre-existence and state of being prior to his incarnation as "the Word became flesh" (John 1:14). This first strophe (v. 6) details his mindset as he faced his birth as the God-man: He "did not consider equality with God" something to seize for his own advantage. Paul uses the Greek participle *hyparchōn* (NIV, "being"), which many scholars read in a concessive sense, meaning "*although* he was in very nature[4] God" and showing the extent to which Christ disregarded his divine status when he became human. However, it may be better to take *hyparchōn* as a causal participle: "*because* he was in very nature

---

3. There is no doubt in my mind that this passage is a hymn, but whether Paul wrote it himself or borrowed an existing creedal hymn cannot be known for certain. Either option is possible.

4. Literally, "in the form of God," a Jewish concept meaning that in every way Jesus was divine and manifested the glory of God (John 1:14; Heb 1:3). It combines the idea of external appearance and the substantive reality underlying that appearance.

God," Christ did not have to demand that the world celebrate his status and willingly took the path of servanthood. I have gone back and forth on this issue, but at present I slightly prefer a causal understanding.

This is a critical passage on the deity of Christ. Paul means that Christ, with his Father (and the Spirit), was an eternal being and that, as such, Jesus was "God of very God," as the Nicene Creed so aptly puts it. Jesus as a member of the Trinity had no beginning and no end (Heb 7:3). He was not created; he was the Creator (John 1:3-5; Col 1:16; Heb 1:2).

The statement on "equality with God" parallels the meaning of "the form of God," but the context is completely different. The "form of God" describes Christ's being in his heavenly existence, while "equality with God" considers this from the perspective of his earthly status. His divine nature continues but in a different context, and in a different relationship with the reality surrounding it. The phrase "to be equal with God" refers to the temptation to demand that all the world recognize his greatness and fall down in worship. This would be the significance of the testing of God's Son in Matthew 4 / Luke 4, where the devil tempted Jesus to seek the world's acknowledgement of his status as the Son of God rather than to accept his destiny as the Suffering Servant. Jesus refused to seek human glory and took the "form" of a slave, leaving the glory up to God for a later time.

Another issue must be discussed, as many have seen a Christ/Adam contrast in this first strophe. In the creation story of Genesis 2-3 Adam was created in the image of God but yielded to temptation and tried to make himself equal with God by eating the forbidden fruit of knowledge, thereby becoming a sinner. Adam was not equal to God but sought to seize that prerogative for himself; in contrast, Christ *was* equal to God but refused to seize that entitlement for himself. The contrast seems clear at a theological level, but the problem is that Paul gives no hint of an Adamic theme or of parallels with Genesis 2-3. This discussion would make for a great sermon theme, paralleling the so-called "Adam **Christology**" of Romans 5:12–21 or 1 Corinthians 15:45–49. Still, while this makes a lot of sense, we cannot be certain Paul had any such thing in mind. I remain interested but not convinced.

There are equally important issues with regard to the meaning of "used to his own advantage" (Greek: *harpagmon*). This could be active in force—an act of robbery (as in the KJV) or of seizing a thing for oneself—or passive in effect—something to be retained (based on the tendency for the Greek suffixes -*mos* and -*ma* to indicate a passive form). In the first interpretation Christ is tempted to grab his glory for himself; in the second he is tempted to desire recognition of his glory from those around him. In both cases Christ possesses the divine glory but refuses the earthly glory. The only question is whether the temptation was to forcefully seize it or to passively desire the worship of others.

There is a growing consensus, reflected in the NIV, that the best way forward is to see an active sense but to understand it in a more abstract way—that Christ was indeed "God of very God" and knew it, but that he refused to exploit his glory and "take advantage" of it for his own gain. This leads well into the next strophe/verse, which shows him taking the lowly place of a slave. The humility of Christ runs completely counter to the self-aggrandizement of the rulers of history—as well as to the mindset of people today who reverse the golden rule, saying in effect, "Do unto others before they can get a chance to do unto you!" The American way is to grab all the glory, prestige, and goodies for oneself. Jesus demonstrated another way.

Christ's state of being—made himself nothing (2:7)

This second strophe depicts the action Christ took to demonstrate his refusal to take advantage of his glory and power. It is his completely startling decision to "empty himself" (Greek: *heauton ekenōsen*). The meaning of this has fueled vociferous debates for centuries. This is partly due to what has been called the "kenotic heresy," a view that Jesus emptied himself of his divinity when he became human. Few interpreters have gone to such an extreme, for that view doesn't fit the hymn itself, let alone the New Testament's overall teaching on the divinity of Christ (for instance, John 1:1, 14, 18; 10:30; Rom 9:5; Titus 2:13; Heb 1:8; 2 Pet 1:1).

The key issue is whether the hymn is using the literal meaning of the Greek verb *kenoō* ("to empty") or the figurative meaning ("to take the lower place" or "to make of no effect"). In 2:7 the verb has no direct object of content, so Christ did not divest himself *of anything* here. Thus it is far better to see a figurative meaning, as in the KJV ("made himself of no reputation") or NIV ("made himself nothing"). There have been three major theories:

1. A modified kenotic approach—According to this view Jesus divested himself not of his deity but of his divine prerogatives, like omnipotence or omniscience, when he became the God-man. The problem with this is that he still could demonstrate divine power, as in his nature miracles, and omniscience, as in his knowledge about Simon, Nathaniel, and the Samaritan woman (John 1:42, 47–49; 4:16–19). Moreover, as stated above, this verb is likely meant not in a literal but in a figurative sense.

2. Jesus as Suffering Servant—Some say the emphasis here centers not on his incarnation but on the cross (v. 8). Parallels between this passage and the Servant Song of Isaiah 52–53 are used to support this (for instance, "emptied himself" = "poured out his life to death" in 53:12). The parallels are there, as we will see, but they occur later in the hymn rather than here. In verses 6–7, the context definitely supports an incarnational reference. The movement is from Jesus' pre-existent state in heaven (v. 6) to his incarnational state as the God-man (v. 7). Suffering and death enter in verse 8, not in verse 7.

3. The incarnation as the lower place—The figurative thrust supports the general consensus that the hymn stresses

Jesus leaving the glory of his heavenly state and "making himself nothing" by becoming human. This picture is fleshed out in the next two clauses, which tell us *how* Christ made himself nothing (by taking … by becoming).

In his incarnation Christ did not merely become human. Using the language of verse 6, he took on himself "the very nature of a servant." The Greek is "in the form of a slave" and connotes two things. First, the contrast with verse 6 is striking. The One whose very nature was divinity as God is the same One who at his incarnation took on the very nature of a slave, becoming the God-man—fully God and fully human—and then, as the God-man, serving all humanity as its slave who was willing to die on its behalf. There is no way that the human mind can fully grasp this concept; we must accept it by faith.

Second, Christ became not just a servant (Greek: *diakonos*) but a slave (*doulos*, used in v. 7). Many have tied this with the *Ebed Yahweh* ("Servant of the Lord") theology of Isaiah 52–53, and that makes sense; the themes are very much present and will appear several times in the material that follows. But the hymn's use of *doulos* goes much deeper. Christ was not just the Servant of the Lord but had come to serve humankind. He gave up all his rights in order to serve us his whole life and, as will be emphasized below in v. 8b, to die for us. Moreover, he was not just servant, but slave. This accounts for the NIV's rendering, "made himself nothing"; slaves were regarded as not quite human because they were owned by another human being. Jesus gave up all his rights in order to die for us. Still, he did not cease to be God. Rather, as the divine God-man he assumed the form/nature of a slave and served humankind totally by purchasing our freedom from the slavery of sin.

In the second line of verse 7, taking the form of a slave is the means by which Jesus emptied himself. In the third line another "by means of" clause describes the incarnation itself, explaining that Jesus emptied himself by means of "being made in human likeness." The second line describes his inward essence as slavehood, the third his outward appearance as humanity. Furthermore, in verse 6 Christ's state of being as God continues from eternity past, but in this third line of verse 7 his state of being as human begins, as his human body "is made" or created. He *becomes* "in human likeness," as he is made both to resemble humans externally and to be like them internally in terms of his thought processes and emotions. Christ completely identified with all human beings. This is where the mystery of the incarnation comes in—Christ's complete identification with other human beings along with his complete identity with the Godhead. How he could have been fully both is beyond our ken. He gave up nothing of his deity while he assumed all that humanity is—except for one all-important distinction: He did not inherit sin (2 Cor 5:21). As Hebrews 4:15 says so well, he was "just as we are—yet he did not sin."

Christ humbled himself and was crucified (2:8)

This three-line strophe parallels the previous one, and "humbled himself" is defined by "made himself nothing." The means by which Christ did this is found in the first line: "being found in appearance as a man"—that is, through his incarnation. In using the verb "being found" the hymn challenges readers to examine the evidence for themselves and to discover the truth that Jesus was fully human in appearance and yet as the God-man humbled himself as a slave. "Appearance" refers to the outward semblance of a thing, the way it is perceived by the senses. Taken with "found," Paul's meaning is that everyone who examined Jesus knew him to be fully human. With "man," the phrase simply means that as people looked on him they saw a male person.

This fully human male could have secured for himself great glory and fame (as recognized in v. 6) but instead surrendered the accolades and "humbled himself." Now we enter the world of the *Ebed Yahweh* (Servant of the Lord) in Isaiah 52–53. We have already noted the great definition of humility in 2:3, above: Value others above yourself and center on their needs and interests above your own. This humbling is not limited to the incarnation but defines the entire earthly existence of Christ, culminating in his death, as stated in the next line. It depicts not just his humble mindset and acts of humility, but also his humiliation, as seen in his rejection by his own people, the Jews, and his suffering and crucifixion. As in Isaiah 53:7–8, "He was oppressed and afflicted; ... he was led like a lamb to the slaughter. ... By oppression and judgment he was taken away. ... For the transgression of my people he was punished."

Paul goes on to explore the extent of Christ's self-humiliation: Christ humbled himself "by becoming obedient to death"—an echo of Isaiah 53:12, "he poured out his life unto death." It is interesting that the text does not say to whom Christ was obedient. Certainly God is implied, as in Hebrews 10:7, 9: "Here I am ... I have come to do your will, my God" (from Ps 40:6–8). But the hymn likely goes further and pictures Christ's obedience to his destiny, the reason he became incarnate: his death on the cross. Obviously the two are interdependent, since the Father established the destiny of the Son. "To death" is a strong phrase that uses the Greek preposition *mechri*, meaning "to the point of death" and showing the extent or degree of Christ's obedience.

The Suffering Servant humbled himself and became obedient all the way to his willingness to die for humanity. The end of strophe 3 clarifies this by adding "even death on the cross," which brings the first half of the hymn to a climax. It is one thing to die an honorable death but quite another to die the most humiliating, degrading death imaginable. Scholars have long recognized that there was no more cruel, horrendous way to die in all the ancient world than crucifixion. This was the archetypal act of humility and obedience to the divine calling—Jesus' atoning sacrifice of himself on the cross. The mind-boggling truth is that the Father and the Son chose this as the way Jesus had to die, and he voluntarily placed himself on the cross in order to atone for our sins!

It is important to note the absolute contrast between the deep humility of Jesus depicted in this hymn and the arrogance Paul describes in verse 2. Against the backdrop of people filled with "vain conceit" and the desire for glory, Christ surrendered his glory and "made himself nothing." The polar opposite of being consumed by "selfish ambition," Jesus made himself a slave to serve every created being. Whereas people's natural tendency is to focus on their own desires, Jesus thought only of others and their needs. They wanted it all, and Jesus died for *them*! There could be no greater model of humility in the history of this world.

CHRIST'S STATE OF EXALTATION (2:9–11)

Christ is the subject of verses 6–8 and acts entirely in a self-humbling direction. God the Father, on the other hand, is the subject of verses 9–11, and Christ is the recipient. God now acts to pour out glory and honor on his Son. The theme is powerful: Jesus seeks humility, refuses glory, and takes the lowest place at his incarnation, and the Father exalts and glorifies his Son at his ascension. Jesus makes himself the Suffering Servant who dies for the salvation of sinful humankind, while God declares him *Christus Victor* (Latin: "the victorious Christ") and makes all creation fall at his feet, either in worship or in forced surrender. Christ comes as slave and ultimately becomes Lord of all. Here is the model for us. If we emulate Christ's humble mindset, God will glorify us and allow us to share in the glory of the Son (see 3:20, below).

His exaltation by God (2:9)

The opening "therefore" shows that the next three strophes/verses are the direct consequence and result of Christ's self-abasement in verses 6–8. His humiliation leads directly to his exaltation. His action is now joined by his Father's action. In actuality, the glory the Father now gives the Son is not a new status but a return to his former, pre-existent glory (as seen in v. 6). This is the same as in the transfiguration, where Christ's radiance was not a new phenomenon but his pre-existent splendor breaking forth and shining through his earthly, human body. Jesus' entire life, from incarnation to death, was a self-humiliation, and God was now reversing all of his servanthood actions and returning to him his eternal glory. This was not a reward for Jesus' self-denial; there was no merit theology at work, for God was returning to Jesus that glory which had always been his. Still, from our perspective there is a bestowal on Jesus of status and glory that were never recognized during his earthly life. This is the vantage point of the hymn.

At Jesus' death God decisively intervened and turned everything around. The seeming defeat of the cross now became the cosmic victory of Jesus over all the forces of evil. Let us rehearse these final events from a heavenly perspective. Satan had entered Judas and acted powerfully to send Jesus to the cross, as Jesus says in John 14:30, but in actuality Satan's action was to become his own great defeat (John 12:31; 16:11). The moment Jesus died, he proclaimed to the demonic realm its collapse (1 Pet 3:19); then he disarmed the cosmic powers and led them in his victory procession through the heavens as he ascended to his Father (Col 2:15).

At that moment God affirmed Christ's eternal victory and "exalted him to the highest place." In Ephesians 1:20 Paul describes this as God raising him from the dead and seating "him at his right hand in the heavenly realms," fulfilling Psalm 110:1.[5] In the Greek text the featured word is *hyper* ("above"), which occurs twice ("highest place" and "above every name") and is closely connected to the basic meaning of "exalted" as "lifting up above" all things. All three passion predictions in the Gospel of John feature "lifted up" sayings that mean, in effect, "to lift up Jesus

---

5. Psalm 110:1: "The LORD says to my lord, 'Sit at my right hand until I make your enemies a footstool for your feet.'"

on the cross is to lift him up into glory" (John 3:14; 8:28; 12:32); these sayings attest that, in reality, the cross was where Jesus was enthroned as royal Messiah. He was elevated not above his own pre-existing glory but, in an elative sense, to the highest possible position as Lord of all. He had surrendered that position in his incarnation, but in his exaltation he returned to his earlier glory.

To clarify the meaning of Christ's exaltation, the next line adds that at this event God "gave him the name that is above every name." This shows the extent of his glorified status, signifying sovereign control over all creation. Adam's naming of the animals in Genesis 2:20 represented his dominion over the animal world. So here, the hymn proclaims Jesus' dominion over the cosmos, as expressed in Colossians 1:15–16 ("firstborn over all creation"; "all things have been created through him and for him"). In Philippi—a Roman garrison city that celebrated its close relationship to Caesar as Lord—it was a powerful (and quite dangerous) witness to declare that Christ Jesus, not Caesar, was the true Lord.

The consensus view is that the "name" given to Jesus is "LORD" (a common substitute for "Yahweh," in order to avoid uttering the divine name). This alludes to Isaiah 45:23–24: "Before me every knee will bow; by me every tongue will swear. They will say of me, 'In the LORD alone are deliverance and strength.'" Yahweh had conferred on Jesus his own covenant name, as recognized in the "I AM" sayings of John 8:24, 28, 58; 13:19, echoing the "I AM" of Isaiah 43:10; 47:8, 10.[6] This is both a name and a title, indicating that Jesus is a member of the Triune Godhead named "Yahweh," as well as Lord of all creation. The Suffering Servant is now proclaimed to be the sovereign Lord.

---

6. See also Isaiah 41:13; 42:8; 43:11; 45:5, 18.

His exaltation via worship and submission (2:10)

The fifth strophe begins with *hina* ("so that"), which normally indicates purpose but here may point to the result of Christ's exaltation, setting up the next two verses. "At the name of Jesus" places the emphasis on his earthly life and ministry. His humiliation, atoning work, and exaltation revealed him as the Perfect Man. His accomplishment as the God-man provides the ground and reason for the worship expressed in these last two strophes (verses 10-11). The "name" stands for the character and person of Jesus in all he has done. Still, this does not mean "the name 'Jesus'" but more likely "the name Jesus was given"—that is, "Lord"/"Yahweh." The Son accomplished his redemptive work as Jesus and was vindicated and acknowledged as Lord of the universe.

The result of the exaltation of Jesus as Lord is both submission and worship: "Every knee should bow." This depicts all of creation kneeling before Christ—the saints in adoration and worship and the sinners and the demonic realm in forced homage and submission. This too alludes to Isaiah 45:23: "Before me every knee will bow, by me every tongue will swear." In Isaiah this statement celebrates the victory of Yahweh over the nations, while here it details the submission and worship of creation to its Creator. Also in Isaiah, God is acknowledged by all as Creator and as the only God: "I am the Lord, and there is no other" (45:18). The hymn applies both affirmations—Creator and only God—to Jesus. He is the Lord God to whom every knee will bow.

It is difficult to determine whether the hymn celebrates the worship of Christ by animate and inanimate creation or whether the focus is on created beings who bow the knee and confess with their mouth. The key is whether the Greek terms in the third line, "in heaven and on earth and under the earth," are masculine or neuter (in their grammatical gender). A reference to the whole of creation would make a great deal of sense here. However, in light of these last two strophes, and in keeping with Isaiah 45, it is better to see verses 10–11 as referring to sentient beings who voluntarily bow in adoration and submission to Christ, the Victor. Those in heaven would be the angelic beings who inhabit heaven, those on earth would be human beings, and those under the earth likely include both departed humans and the demonic realm. All created beings will join together, some in joy and others in defeat, to bow before the Lord of the universe—the Triune Godhead, but here especially Christ Jesus.

His exaltation via confession (2:11)

Again drawn from Isaiah 45:23, this verse adds confession with the mouth to obeisance with the knee. The Greek word *exomologeō* is a strong verb referring to public confession, and while it does mean to "acknowledge" a person, it goes beyond that. In the **Septuagint** (the Greek translation of the Old Testament) *exomologeō* nearly always speaks of praise and thanksgiving (1 Chr 29:13; Pss 7:17; 30:4) and connotes joyous confession. This produces a difficulty, for clearly the emphasis is on *all* of creation—including the sinners and the cosmic powers. Yet how can the enemies of God joyously confess him? Due to this tension some scholars interpret the verb simply as "acknowledge" (with the NIV); however, I feel that the tension should be allowed to stand. The opponents of God and of his people will be the conquered who are forced to acknowledge Jesus' lordship, while the rest of creation will joyfully praise him.

The focus of both verses 10 and 11 is on the next line: "that Jesus Christ is Lord." This climaxes the entire hymn, returning to the reality that the pre-existent glory of the One whose very nature is divinity continues to shine in Jesus, who is Lord of all and Yahweh himself. His is truly the name that is above every name, although there remains a name yet to be revealed, as in Revelation 19:12: "a name written on him that no one knows but he himself." There is a final reality, a revelation of God's being that cannot be made known until that ultimate phase of eternity has begun. This is closely related to another early confession, "O Lord, come" (1 Cor 16:22)—a prayer for the return of Christ when all of creation will acknowledge him publicly and joyously: "Jesus Christ is Lord."

The purpose of it all is captured in the last line, "to the glory of God the Father." This is a frequent emphasis in Paul's letters; in the prologue of Ephesians, for example, "the praise of his glorious grace" is stressed at key points detailing the spiritual gifts distributed to the saints (Eph 1:3, 6, 12, 14). Here in Philippians 2 the whole of the hymn is in mind. Jesus' incarnation (when he "made himself nothing"), his sacrificial death on the cross, and his exaltation to universal lordship and acclamation by all creation all redound to the glory of God. Nothing should be excluded.

The emphasis here on the fatherhood of God appears at two other places in Philippians (1:3; 4:20), and all three statements occur in a creedal context highlighting God's intimate relationship with his children, whom he has redeemed and adopted (Rom 8:14-17). Think about it: God knew when he created humankind that he would have to redeem these beings who would fall into sin. In his omniscience he was fully aware of the terrible price he would have to pay for creation. Yet his love was so great that he willingly paid the cost and purchased our redemption. How could that not lead to praise and glory? God is in the process of bringing this sinful world to its culmination. Romans 8:18-22 speaks of creation as "subject to frustration" and as eagerly awaiting its release at the **eschaton** (end of the present age). Thus all of creation, along with us, will be praising and glorifying the exalted Lord and bringing glory to God. Christ's assumption of lordship reveals God anew as the loving Father who has brought his salvation to his beleaguered people.

Many interpreters believe that Christ's model for us is seen in Philippians 2:6-8 but not in verses 9-11. This is not true. The theme of the whole hymn is: "Be like Jesus; seek humility, and leave the glory to God." This passage is closely related to Colossians 3:1–4, probably written less than a year earlier. We who have been raised with Christ must seek the things of heaven rather than the things of earth. When Christ appears we will "appear with him in glory." We must not seek our own earthly glory but await our heavenly glory. That is the message here as well. The believers at Philippi are to live lives of humility and wait as Jesus did for the glory God will give his people at the time he will designate.

———

We must understand this marvelous hymn at both levels of its intended meaning. First, it is a christological masterpiece, defining in succinct yet incredibly deep clauses the true nature and mindset of the Christ, the Son of God, as he became incarnate as the God-man. He took the lowest place imaginable, not just that of a human being but of a slave. He was born for the purpose of dying as the Suffering Servant of Yahweh for the sins of humanity. God the Father then vindicated and exalted Jesus to the highest station as Lord of all, reigning over both the heavenly realm and the created universe. All of his creation confessed and acknowledged him as Lord, and God was glorified.

At the second level, Paul is using this incredible hymn of self-abasement as the archetypal model for all God's people, who like Jesus are never to seek status or self-glory but are to devote their lives to serving others. They must pursue only the good of those around them, while waiting on the Lord—as Jesus did—for vindication and blessing. There can be no conflict or division in a church when the members care little for their own needs but seek always to benefit others, never considering themselves more highly than they should but using all their gifts to serve others.

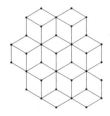

CALL TO OBEDIENCE, HARMONY, AND PURITY

(2:12–18)

In response to the problem of dissension (introduced in 2:1-4), Paul has provided his great example, the incarnate Christ (2:5-11). This continues the theme of the section that began at 1:27: "Whatever happens, conduct yourselves in a manner worthy of the gospel of Christ." As the messianic community of God, believers are obligated to the gospel both internally, as a united people, and externally, as a witnessing people. In both areas their inner cohesion as the body of Christ is essential. The Christ-hymn exemplified how this can be achieved—through humility and servanthood—and in this light Paul now addresses further the problem of the Philippians' dissension. This draws together the pride of those in 2:1-4 and the humility of Christ in verses 6-8, brokering the conclusion that there is no room in the church for "grumbling or arguing" (v. 14). Like Christ, his followers are to shine in this dark world as "stars in the sky" (v. 15).

PAUL DEMANDS THAT THEY
BE OBEDIENT (2:12-13)

Their Part—Work Out Their Salvation (2:12)

"Therefore" draws a conclusion from the whole of 1:27–2:11 but especially from the model of Christ in 2:5–11. Paul often calls his readers "my dear friends" when he is giving them important admonitions (Rom 12:19; 1 Cor 10:14; 2 Cor 7:1). He felt especially close to the Philippians and wanted them to know that his concerns stemmed from his deep love for them (expressed in 1:8). He appealed to their lengthy and glorious history of "obedience" to the gospel and the demands of the Lord; from the founding of the church until the present day they had been known for their Christian faithfulness. Most likely that included obedience to Paul's apostolic teaching. Christ was "obedient to death—even death on a cross" (2:8), and believers were to follow his paradigm in their own lives. The importance of obedience is a frequent motif in Paul's letters, as in Romans 1:5 ("obedience that comes from faith"), Romans 6:16 ("obedience which leads to righteousness"), and 2 Corinthians 10:5 ("take captive every thought to make it obedient to Christ"). The idea of obedience and the exhortation here to "work out your salvation" are interconnected; both reinforce the governing theme of this section, expressed in 1:27, to "walk worthily of the gospel." The Christian life is to be worked out in obedience to the will of God, as expressed in his word.

Moreover, the Philippians no longer had Paul's presence among them, as he was in prison for Christ, and it therefore had become even more critical for them to live lives of obedience in Paul's absence. He often spoke of being "absent in the body, present in spirit" (1 Cor 5:3; Col 2:5; 1 Thess 2:17), and the idea is the same here. Paul could not be with them to encourage and stimulate their obedience to the Lord, helping them to overcome their animosity and find unity once again in their church. So it was all the more important that they remember their past faithfulness to the Lord and work all the harder to remain obedient to their heavenly calling. They would have to solve their personal crises and find their way back to oneness.

All of this prepares the way for Paul's primary exhortation: "Continue to work out your salvation (Greek: *sōtēria*) with fear and trembling." There has been considerable discussion about the meaning of this command. At the outset we must be clear that Paul is not speaking of initial salvation as conversion. He could hardly be saying "save yourself," for he consistently stresses that salvation in this sense is a gift of God and not a reward earned by personal merit (Eph 2:8–9). Some interpreters see the focus as individual salvation, centering on a person's Christian life as a whole, and others as corporate salvation, centering on the life of the church. The former view aligns with the meaning of salvation in Paul's other writings, but latter fits closely with the surrounding context in Philippians and the problem of church dissension. In recent years the corporate view has gained support. In secular Greek, *sōtēria* often could describe the health and well-being of a person or a group, and 1:27–2:18 is certainly a corporate context calling for unity and spiritual healing; moreover, the commands are plural, addressing all the believers at Philippi. On the other hand, there are good grounds for a personal thrust. In Paul's letters *sōtēria* nearly always means spiritual salvation (Rom 1:16; Eph 1:13; Phil 1:28). While this does not refer only to the original conversion experience, it does refer to the working out of the believers' salvation vis-à-vis their ongoing Christian conduct. In the New Testament, *sōtēria* connotes the life in Christ as a whole, including sanctification as well as regeneration. So the plural commands here do not necessarily refer to the church as a whole but to all the people in the church.

In reality it is an error to make this an either/or; it is a both/and. Paul was instructing every member of the Philippian church to work out the implications of their own salvation or life with God by working with the other members to achieve peace and harmony within their church. It is essential for every believer to work at their Christian walk as part of the corporate body of Christ. Interpreters generally agree that there is an **eschatological** element in this—that believers are to live in the present in light of the future end of history, when Christ will return and abolish this age of sin and discord. For Paul the future began with the present moment: "Now is the time of God's favor; now is the day of salvation" (2 Cor 6:2). His readers, then and now, are the messianic community, and the day of salvation has already begun. Now we must live like it. We are not just responsible to one another to end conflict and bring love back to center stage in our church life. We are responsible to Christ, to whom we will give account for our actions (Rom 14:12; 2 Cor 5:10; Heb 13:17). This is the reason for "with fear and trembling." The Greek term *phobos* refers to both awe and fear. It is common to interpret Paul's meaning here as reverential awe, and while that is certainly part of the thrust the inclusion of "trembling" has to involve more than reverence. In the Old Testament, this word pair normally depicted the terror and dread of people who were facing God, like the Canaanites (Exod 15:16; Deut 2:25) or the Egyptians (Isa 2:19). So while Paul is definitely speaking of a worshipful awe as we live out our lives before God, he also looks to the fear with which we carry out our responsibilities before God.

Our Christian life matters, and our actions have eternal consequences. The warning of 2 Timothy 2:15 is appropriate: "Do your best to present yourself to God as one approved, a workman who does not need to be ashamed." The Philippians did not want to stand before God in shame for failing to resolve their selfish discord and find harmony. There is a mixture of reverential awe and serious responsibility toward God's will as we work out the implications of our eternal salvation in our daily lives.

GOD'S PART—WORKING IN THEM (2:13)

Linking verses 12-13 with the Greek word *gar* ("for"), Paul clarifies that the work of developing our salvation or walk with Christ is not an isolated act on our part; it is grounded in and made possible by the greater reality that God is at work in us. We do not rely on our own strength but are "strong in the Lord and in his mighty power" (Eph 6:10). The Greek verb for "works" in verse 13 is *energeō*, whose English derivative, "energy," provides a good conception of God's mighty action as he empowers and enables us to work at our Christian walk. In other words, God "energizes" us as we face the daunting task of living rightly in an evil world.

These two verses describe a truly wondrous process that defines successful Christian living: As we work at our salvation or Christian responsibilities we don't have to worry about whether we will have sufficient strength or wisdom to make the right decisions and put them to work in our daily lives, for God is at work undergirding us with his greater strength. This is expressed well in Isaiah 40:27-31: When we grow weary and are weak the tireless God will pour his own strength into us. All we need to do is "wait on the Lord," and we will receive a brand new strength—his own—so that we can "soar on wings like eagles" and walk with new power in our lives. We are required to exhibit an active trust and to work hard at casting off the old self and putting on the new (Rom 6:4-6; Eph 4:22-24), but it is God who empowers us to do so.

The object of God's continuous work in our lives is "to will and to act in order to fulfill his good purpose." There is some question as to whether God works *his* will and *his* work in us, or whether he is at work empowering us so that *our* will and *our* work will fulfill his purposes in us. The latter reading is almost certainly Paul's emphasis here. Both of the infinitive verbs used here ("to will" and "to act") are present tense, indicating believers' ongoing willing and acting to serve God. God works in us to bring our will into alignment with his will, so that we can work not to get ahead in this world but rather to "fulfill his good purpose" for us. This means both to meet his "purposes" and to bring him "pleasure." We are called to seek at all times to please God in our lives and to do that which is acceptable to him.

PAUL COMMENDS THE PATH OF HARMONY AND PURITY (2:14-16A)

The Refusal to Complain or Argue (2:14)

Verses 14-16 form a single complicated sentence in which Paul applies all he has said in verses 6-11 and 12-13 to the situation at Philippi. As the believers there worked out their Christian walk in the life of their church, the first characteristic they needed to pursue was a peaceful heart. Both inside and outside the church, their relationships and their witness to Christ were at stake. Paul begins with a wide-sweeping injunction: "Do everything" incorporates every area of life, both the sacred and the secular aspects. It includes both the willing and the working of verse 13. Everything had to be done without "grumbling or arguing," in the attitude of genuine servanthood Paul describes throughout this chapter.

There is a clear allusion here to the Israelites' complaining in the wilderness, when their continual bickering and grumbling against God brought down his wrath on their heads (Exod 16:6-12; Num 14:27-30; 21:4-5). This negative example was often used in the early church to warn Christians about such attitudes (1 Cor 10:10-12; Heb 3:7-19). However, while some believers at Philippi apparently were quarreling with each other, there is no evidence that they were grumbling against God. Most likely, Paul is saying that disputes in the community are tantamount to complaints against God (for whatever is done against God's people is, in effect, done against God). In the time of the exodus, grumbling against Moses was taken as complaining against God (Exod 16:2; Num 14:2). The same is true in Philippi. When negative attitudes drive relationships in the body of Christ, the problem will be deemed a failure before God, and the church's witness will be compromised.

THE PURPOSE—TO SHINE LIKE STARS (2:15–16A)

A pure people in a crooked world (2:15)

If the believers allowed dissension to rear its ugly head, they could not be "blameless and pure." So it was imperative that they rid themselves of any argumentative spirit and eschew all divisive complaints in the church. God has placed his people in this sinful world, and the world must see how different they are. Their very witness is at stake, for the world will see little reason to affiliate with a divided church. God wants his followers to be a beacon of hope and light in a dark and hopeless world.

To define what believers are to be, Paul uses three Greek terms, all beginning with the *a*- of negation: *amemptoi* (without blame), *akeraioi* (without any flaw), and *amōma* (without fault). These words are used in the **Septuagint** (the Greek translation of the Old Testament) to describe the perfect sacrifice offered up to God. Here in Philippians they describe the "children of God"— those who by means of their conversion have been made a new creation and a new humanity (Col 2:14–15), members of a new family. They cry out "Abba, Father" (Rom 8:14–17; Gal 4:6), and so they must act like God's children in their relationships with one another. Quarreling and complaining are faults that must be abandoned so the family of God can shine forth and draw the world to itself. God's children are to be "perfect" and whole as they represent their perfect Father to the world.

The world in which God has placed his people is "a warped and crooked generation," Paul says. He is quoting here from the Septuagint's translation of the Song of Moses, which describes the faithless Israelites as "disgraced children, … a rebellious and perverted generation" (Deut 32:5). It is difficult to know for certain how to apply this to Philippians, for Paul in this passage is speaking of the pagan world, not Israel. Most likely he means that unbelieving Israel had lost its identity and become like the unbelieving nations. Thus, his point centers on the warped minds and crooked morals of the unsaved world. Such corruption also pervades our present time, as is plain to see: Just watch the news, go to the movies, or read a modern novel.

The church, composed of believing Jews and Gentiles, is the new Israel, the true people of God. Consequently, the body of Christ is to be the polar opposite of the wilderness generation—pure rather than warped, blameless rather than crooked. The new Israel will continue God's original purpose in choosing Israel, serving as "a light for the Gentiles" (Isa 49:6). The character of this crooked world is described in Romans 1:21: "Their thinking became futile and their foolish hearts were darkened." God has placed his people in the midst of this sin-sick world so that his truth may rescue these perishing people. Through the witness of the church, "the light shines in the darkness" (John 1:5), but it is essential that the purity of that witness be maintained. As Paul puts it here, "Then you will shine among them like stars in the sky." Jesus is the "light of the world" (John 8:12), and his followers are called to be the same (Matt 5:14). In college I spent a semester as a student missionary in Pakistan and, with another missionary, went trekking in the foothills of the Himalayas. Every night I would have a hard time falling asleep because of the beauty of the millions of stars shining as I had never before seen them. I couldn't tear my eyes away from the display. Believers are to shine so brightly that the people of the world are mesmerized, but that will not happen if the lens of our witness is marred by petty bickering. We are light-bearers, and through us the light of God must radiate forth and fill the sky with the beauty of God. Paul challenges us here to be united in the beauty and glory of our witness.

Holding firm to the gospel (2:16a)

Note the progression of thought in 2:14-16. Paul was exhorting these Christians to maintain a pure witness in the world. This demanded that they desist from their shallow complaints and self-centered arguing. Paul was describing what a true family of God should look like. There are two characteristics here: a shining witness (v. 15) and a firm stance centered on the Word (v. 16). These are interdependent: In the first characteristic the gospel is proclaimed to a dying world, while in the second it is defended against the false charges of an unbelieving world. The goal of the first is life for the world and of the second the truth of the Word.

The thought goes back to 1:27-30, where Paul tells the Philippians to "stand firm in the one Spirit" and not to allow themselves to be "frightened in any way by those who oppose you." Ours is a fearless stance based on the eternal truths of God. The gospel reality here is called "the word of life" in the sense that it brings God's life to a dying world. The more I teach the Bible in a diversity of contexts, the more I ask myself how anyone could fail to be excited by the treasures and richness of the Word that God has revealed to us. Would any famous person ever think that I am important enough to sit down and share their wisdom with me? Probably not, but God does! Bible study is the true treasure hunt, and what we dig up in this search for true riches will enrich us for eternity. That is a reality on which we can stand firm!

THE PHILIPPIAN CHURCH IS
PAUL'S LEGACY (2:16B-18)

Paul Desires to Boast Because
of the Philippians (2:16b)

In the second half of verse 16, Paul is saying that his very pride is at stake in the Philippians' acquiescence to his exhortations: "And then I will be able to boast on the day of Christ." This is actually a purpose clause: "I tell you this *so that* I may boast." The "day of Christ" is the Old Testament "day of the Lord," the end of history. It signifies the return of Christ, that time when we will receive our resurrection bodies and also our rewards. At that time we will all give account of our life and ministry to the Lord. In Philippians 4:1 Paul calls the Philippians "my joy and crown," and when that is linked with the idea of "boasting" he is saying in effect, "I want to be proud of you when I meet the Lord." When we boast about ourselves it is sin; when we boast about others, on the other hand, and especially about the things of God, we are manifesting a natural joy and pride in what really matters.

When we stand before the Lord we will give an account not only for our personal lives but also for our efforts in ministry. I will be judged on the quality of my life as a husband and father, as well as on the quality of my ministry. This is why Paul challenged Timothy in 2 Timothy 2:15 to work hard to be approved and to avoid being ashamed. Paul is reflecting the same concept here. He wanted assurance that in his ministry at Philippi he "did not run or labor in vain"—in other words, that there was no lack of results from his work in their church.

Paul is using two metaphors: (1) athletic imagery, describing the race of life in order to depict the great effort needed to finish well in ministry (see 1 Cor 9:24-26; Gal 2:2; 2 Tim 2:5; Heb 12:1-3); and (2) the image of manual labor and the hard work needed to make a living. In both images Paul depicts a great deal of effort, potentially with no gain to show for it. If the Philippians were to self-destruct, all of Paul's efforts would have been for naught, and he would be filled with shame when he stood before the Lord. His prayer was that this outcome would not come to pass, that these people would indeed respond, find healing before the Lord, and become the light-bearing witness in Philippi they were meant to be.

PAUL'S DRINK OFFERING AND MUTUAL REJOICING (2:17–18)

Paul now shifts the imagery and depicts his work on behalf of the Philippians as a drink offering. This metaphor would have been recognizable in both pagan and Jewish contexts. The Romans would pour a portion of wine onto the ground as a libation to the gods, and the Jews would combine the drink and burnt offerings in the sense of sharing a meal with God in his house/temple.

In referring to a sacrifice to God, Paul probably had in mind three different levels: (1) primarily, his possible execution (after the decision in his trial is handed down), representing a drink offering as his blood is poured out in sacrifice for the Philippians to God; (2) the suffering and sacrifices Paul had been making in his ministry, as he ran and labored (v. 16) for the believers' sakes; and (3) the Philippians' sacrificial service for God. The first two levels belong together. Paul was thinking of his many years of suffering and service in his apostolic ministry, but his present-tense statement ("I am being poured out as a drink offering") especially points to the culmination of his ministry in possible martyrdom. Note the parallel in 2 Timothy 4:6: "I am already being poured out like a drink offering, and the time for my departure is near." Paul was uncertain whether he would be executed and actually believed he would be released (1:25), but either way he was pouring himself out on behalf of the Philippians. Here he is saying that "even if" his life of sacrificial service were to end in the near future with his death, he would rejoice in the privilege of serving the Philippian church. This is a beautiful and powerful message. If Paul were asked to pour out his life's blood for the cause of Christ, he would joyfully consider this a drink offering to God. In the same way the drink offering completed the sacrifice, his death would complete his sacrificial service of ministry for the believers' sakes.

The third level in the sacrificial imagery comes in the phrase "on the sacrifice and service coming from your faith." Paul was pouring himself out for the Philippians as they were pouring themselves out for God. Later in this letter, he speaks of their sacrificial service both to himself and to God (2:30; 4:18), so his point is that he would gladly give his life for these people who were faithfully serving the Lord. As a drink offering, his sacrifice would complete both his sacrificial service and their own. The Philippians' service was two-fold, encompassing their faithful witness in hostile surroundings (1:27–30) as well as the gifts they had sent to Paul (4:14–18). They had served him and the Lord in both ways, and he was grateful. He viewed their life of faith and service as an acceptable sacrifice to God and saw himself as privileged to offer his sacrificial ministry—and perhaps his life—as a libation to God, completing the believers' faithful service.

In light of this shared sacrifice, there was mutual joy, which Paul expresses as strongly as possible: "I am glad and rejoice with all of you. So you too should be glad and rejoice with me." He could have said simply "Let's rejoice together," but he wanted to be as comprehensive and emphatic as he could. The first sentence calls for rejoicing with respect to the believers' situation at Philippi, the second with respect to Paul's circumstances in Rome.

———

Whatever transpires, God's people are *called to joy*—which would make a good title for Paul's letter to the Philippians. The idea actually flows from a theology of suffering, as every trial that tests our faith provides a cause for rejoicing (Jas 1:2; 1 Pet 1:6). We can have joy in our hardships because we know that God is sovereign over all our circumstances and will turn everything around for our good (Rom 8:28; the whole of Heb 11). The key is the difference between happiness and rejoicing. We are happy when things are going the way we like, but we are not expected to be happy in painful experiences (Heb 12:11). Joy, on the other hand, is based on the presence of God and his eschatological promises. So when trials come we might not be happy, but we certainly rejoice, having confidence in God's goodness and faithfulness to us.

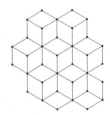

COMMENDING TIMOTHY AND EPAPHRODITUS

(2:19–30)

At first glance this is a very strange section, one we would expect at the end of the letter (as in Romans 16) but not in its middle. Moreover, when Paul describes the work of an associate he normally devotes a verse or two to the subject (as in Col 1:7–8) but not twelve verses, as here. This sort of material is often referred to as a "travelogue," a paragraph detailing the travel plans of Paul and his associates so the readers will be aware of their intended movements. In the case of Philippians, there are two reasons for this information. First, Paul felt that the issues facing this church required urgent personal attention, but he was confined in Rome until his trial was over, so he was planning to send Timothy as his representative. To ensure that the congregation would recognize the authority Timothy had been given, Paul provided in this letter a brief introduction and commendation (a common practice in the ancient world). Second, having just portrayed Christ as an example of the humble-minded servant of God, Paul wanted to present two others—Timothy and Epaphroditus. It took more than a verse or two to develop the paradigm the Philippians could expect to see embodied in these men. So this passage involves not merely mundane personal matters but a critical theme of the letter. The believers already knew Timothy, and Epaphroditus was one of their own. Both men served as ideal models of the kind of behavior Paul wanted to inculcate in this church.

Let's rehearse the situation behind the letter. Paul had probably been in his prison apartment for nearly two years, and his capital trial was nearing its end. Several months earlier, the Philippian church had sent Epaphroditus to Rome to deliver a monetary gift and to help Paul in his ministry. Then several events had happened in succession, including Epaphroditus' serious illness (2:26-27) and Paul's receipt of news about dissension in the church. Paul would like to have gone to Philippi shortly after receiving this report, but the trial was unlikely to wrap up anytime soon. He decided to have Epaphroditus return home—so the believers could see firsthand that he had recovered—and to send Timothy a short while later.

This letter likely was sent with Epaphroditus in order to explain his return to Philippi and to address Paul's concerns about the church there, as well as to lay groundwork for the upcoming visit by Timothy, who would try to rectify the situation among the believers. In this section Paul intended to use both of these coworkers as examples for the Philippians to follow—Timothy as a model of love and concern for others and Epaphroditus as a model of perseverance and integrity in the midst of great personal suffering.

PAUL COMMENDS TIMOTHY FOR HIS DEEP LOVE AND CONCERN (2:19-24)

His Decision to Send Timothy (2:19)

Due to the capital trial situation in Rome Paul knew he could not get to Philippi to address the problems as soon as he would like. He could be executed (2:17), though he expected that God would see to his release (1:25). Still, at the very least it could be a few weeks before he learned the outcome of the trial, and probably even longer before he might actually be released. So his best recourse was to send Timothy as soon as possible and to wait for news, following this up with a personal visit after his release. He says "I hope *in the Lord* to send Timothy to you soon," knowing that all his plans were dependent on God's will. Hope is an **eschatological** term that recognizes the absolute control of the future by God. The secular person can rely on only chance and worldly preparations with regard to the future, but the child of God has an absolute certainty that whatever the future holds will be for the best. Note Paul's emphasis on "the Lord" as the One who has complete, sovereign authority over all future events.

Timothy, a young disciple with a godly mother and grandmother, had joined Paul's team at the beginning of the second missionary journey (Acts 16:1–3). He was the closest thing Paul had to a son, and he had proved invaluable as a coworker. He remained close to Paul, who often sent him to churches as his representative (Berea, Acts 17:14; Thessalonica, 1 Thess 3:2–3; Corinth, 1 Cor 4:17). His purpose here seems to be to inform Paul of the actual situation at Philippi, so that Paul could be "cheered when I receive news about you." This most likely was a two-way street, for in the same way Paul would be encouraged about them they would be encouraged when they learned from Timothy how the trial was going. There is a subtle hint in this, for Paul's "cheer" assumed that the Philippians would solve the problem of their dissension and that Timothy would be able to report back to Paul that they were once again a united and loving congregation.

The Reason—Timothy's Deep Love for Them (2:20–21)

This is a remarkable commendation. Paul in effect puts down his other associates in order to convey the depth of Timothy's love. When he says "I have no one else like him," he has to be including people like Titus, Silas, and Luke. The Greek text actually reads "I have no one of equal soul" (*isopsychon*), meaning "of like soul/mind," extolling Timothy's deep spiritual sensitivity. Paul is likely saying that, of all his associates, no one else so closely approximated his own heart and thinking.

Timothy's "genuine concern for your welfare" would have been the same as Paul's. Timothy was a kindred spirit with Paul, so in sending him Paul felt that he could be present vicariously with the believers. Timothy would be among the Philippian believers as one of the family, demonstrating the same concern and love for the Philippians that Paul would have shown them. Paul could trust that Timothy would ascertain exactly what Paul needed to find out about the situation at Philippi. The Greek term for "concern" (*merimnaō*) is interesting, for it can also refer to anxiety (as in 4:6, "Do not be anxious about anything"). There is a fine line between concern and anxiety, and Paul was certain that Timothy would not cross it. The key was to care deeply, while leaving the outcomes to the Lord and trusting the Spirit's ministry among these believers.

A startling statement comes in verse 21: "For everyone looks out for their own interests, not those of Jesus Christ." There are two difficult questions here. First, does Paul literally mean "everyone"? If so, that would include all of Paul's other associates, among them Barnabas, Luke, and Silas, as well as the twelve apostles. Second, what does Paul mean by "their own interests, not those of Jesus Christ"? This goes back to Paul's definition of humility in 2:3 as "not looking out for their own interests." So is Paul indicting his whole team of coworkers as being carnal Christians? It is generally thought that he is using hyperbole here, or perhaps meaning only those who were with him when he was writing this letter. I do suspect this to be hyperbole, similar to when Jesus said "If anyone comes to me and does not hate father and mother   such a person cannot be my disciple" (Luke 14:26). Jesus was not demanding literal hatred of family but was saying, in effect, that his followers must be so committed to him that their love for their own family is tantamount to hatred in comparison. It is the same here. Timothy was so deeply committed to the Lord and to the Philippians that the rest of Paul's associates paled in comparison. Could it also have been that Paul had tried to get others to go to Philippi but had found no one else willing? That doesn't seem probable, for Timothy would hardly have been Paul's last choice. It is more likely that Paul is using hyperbole to emphasize Timothy's deep commitment to the Lord and to the Philippians. This young protégé was the perfect example of the humble man of God envisioned in 2:3.

TIMOTHY'S FAITHFUL SERVICE WITH PAUL (2:22)

Paul was sending Timothy not only because of his commitment to Christ, but also because he had proven himself to be deeply committed to the service of the gospel. The Philippian believers knew this to be true, a probable reflection of Timothy's ministry alongside Paul when this church was established (Acts 16:16–40). Note how Paul commends Timothy in his letter to the Corinthians: "I sent to you Timothy, my son whom I love, who is faithful in the Lord" (1 Cor 4:17). Similarly, he says here that "as a son with his father he has served with me." Timothy had shown his true character in his unwavering love and loyalty to the ministry he had shared with Paul.

So the Philippians could be sure that when they listened to Timothy they would be listening to the heart of Paul. He was absolutely faithful to Paul's mission as he "served with [Paul] in the work of the gospel." Timothy did not serve Paul, but both served the gospel, and that was what truly mattered. Paul never allowed the focus to be on himself, always redirecting it to Christ Jesus, and that is certainly the case here. The Philippians could trust Timothy, for he was a disciple of Christ, not merely a follower of Paul. Timothy also was a model of servanthood. Unlike some of his colleagues, he refused to seek his own glory, and every part of his ambition was Christ-centered (contrary to the selfish attitude described in 2:3a).

THE TWO "COMINGS" (2:23-24)

In Philippians 2:19 Paul expressed his hope to send Timothy "soon," but now he qualifies that comment and states that he hopes to send him "as soon as I see how things go with me." Obviously Paul is talking about his trial, and he expected the verdict shortly (1:19, 25). Still, he felt that he could not send Timothy to Philippi until he knew the outcome, so Timothy could share the news of the verdict with these anxious believers. It is possible that Timothy had served as a witness for the trial and could not leave until it was over, but we cannot know one way or the other. Some commentators suggest that the "things" to which Paul refers were not so much issues related to the trial as matters of ministry in Rome, perhaps related to the opponents mentioned in 1:15-17. In that case Paul would have needed Timothy to assist him with local issues. However, the language here is very similar to that of 1:12, where "the things concerning me" had to do with his trial. So most likely Paul is speaking here, as well, of the verdict that would determine his fate. As soon as that transpired he would send Timothy.

Paul voices his second "hope" in verse 24, where he shares his "confidence" that he will be freed (also 1:25) and be able to come himself in the near future. He does not clarify how his visit relates to Timothy's, but it seems that he did not believe he would be free to travel to Philippi as soon as he would like. In the meantime he deemed it necessary to send Epaphroditus (with this letter) and Timothy (in a separate journey later on). These arrangements indicate that Paul felt deeply about the challenges at Philippi (primarily the dangers of dissension), considering them so serious as to demand immediate intervention.[1]

The critical phrase is "in the Lord." That is the difference maker. Paul felt quite certain that he would soon be freed because

---

1. It is probable that word had not yet come about the arrival of the Judaizers in Philippi (3:1-4:1). See below on this.

he believed it to be the Lord's will that he be allowed to return to the Philippians, to bring healing to the discord and help them stand firm under the persecution they were enduring. After much prayer, he felt led by the Spirit to make firm plans to help resolve the crises at Philippi. He had planned to travel to Spain and bring the gospel to the western half of the Roman Empire (Rom 15:24), but those plans were on hold due to the problems in Philippi. Dispatching Epaphroditus with this letter and then sending Timothy would be the first steps, after which Paul's personal visit would seal the deal and bring ultimate victory over these issues.

PAUL COMMENDS EPAPHRODITUS FOR HIS FAITHFUL SERVICE (2:25-30)

Epaphroditus[2] had been sent by the Philippian believers to bring their gift to Paul (4:18) and aid him in his work. He had proved an able assistant but at some point had become quite ill, to the point that he had almost died. Aware that news of his grave illness had reached his home church, Epaphroditus had become "distressed" (2:26). Most scholars believe this is why he was sent to Philippi ahead of Timothy. Also, for the reasons stipulated in verse 23 (see above), Timothy could not depart just yet, so the two men would have to make the journey separately. Not wanting to give the impression that Epaphroditus had failed in his mission or was being sent home in disgrace, Paul penned this glowing paean of thanks and commendation.

THE NEED FOR EPAPHRODITUS'S SAKE (2:25-27)

His story—sent to care for Paul (2:25)

Paul's purpose here is to show that Epaphroditus was not returning to Philippi due to any shortcoming on his part. Indeed, he had

---

2. His name is the male form of Aphrodite and means "lovely" or "beautiful."

proven invaluable, but because of the illness he could no longer remain in Rome.

To describe the wonderful ministry Epaphroditus had provided there, Paul uses five terms (the first three of which follow the same order as in Philemon 1–2, written just a few months earlier). Each term portrays Epaphroditus, like Timothy, as a model for the Philippians to emulate:

1. "brother" (Greek: *adelphos*)—Paul uses this term to describe those associates with whom he has an especially close relationship. While he uses the plural form (*adelphoi*, which can mean "brothers" or "brothers and sisters") to describe all believers as a group/family (Phil 1:12, 14; 3:1, 13), the singular form marks a real friendship (Eph 6:21; Col 1:1; 4:9).

2. "co-worker" (*synergos*)—This was not used for any believer in general but was a term like "minister" for those close associates who were part of Paul's ministry team and who traveled with him (when he could) and remained with him for the duration (Rom 16:21; 1 Cor 3:9; Phlm 1, 24). Epaphroditus likely worked with Paul full time and, while in Rome, might have functioned as a kind of district representative from Macedonia.

3. "fellow soldier" (*systratiōtēs*)—This looks at a partner in the ministry in terms of the conflicts and hardships faced. Epaphroditus partnered with Paul in his imprisonment and shared in the difficulties, probably serving as a foot soldier in ministry issues when Paul was unable to travel personally (which obviously would have been most of the time). This term was used of Archippus in Philemon 2, depicting leaders in the church as part of the armies of the Lord of Hosts (= "Lord of Heaven's Armies"). Paul also used this term when he spoke of the sacrifice of God's soldiers (2 Tim 2:3–4) who engaged in spiritual warfare against the powers of darkness (1 Cor 9:7; 2 Cor 10:3; Eph 6:10–12).

4. "messenger" (*apostolos*; related to the Greek verb *apostellō*, "to send")—This term looks especially at Epaphroditus' role as the "one who is sent" by the Philippians to help Paul. In a secondary sense an "apostle" was a person commissioned by an organization as an ambassador to fulfill a task. So Epaphroditus had an official capacity as the representative of the church of Philippi to Paul and the church of Rome.

5. "Sent to take care of my needs"—This phrase translates the Greek word *leitourgos*, which means "minister" or "servant," often referring to priestly ministry in a "liturgical" sense (the transliteration works). Epaphroditus was sent to minister to Paul's needs and to serve his mission in any way he could. Those "needs" certainly included financial support, as seen in 4:18, but Epaphroditus' service went beyond this to all of Paul's needs, both personal and ministry-centered.

These five areas clearly show how Paul intended Epaphroditus to be a paradigm that all the believers could imitate. His comradeship, servant's heart, and ministry sense were all qualities the Philippian church needed in light of the ego and personal-glory issues that were causing problems there. Moreover, he served as an example of how to handle personal suffering, as we will see in the verses that follow.

His distress and serious illness (2:26–27)

In verse 25, Paul lauds Epaphroditus for all that he meant to the team and to Paul himself. Now he turns to the main reason he is writing this passage: Due to the terrible illness Epaphroditus had contracted, Paul was returning him to Philippi.

The difficulty is trying to ascertain what kind of illness this was and why it would have forced Paul to send him home. What sort of "distress" did Epaphroditus feel? Could his "longing" for his friends at home have meant that he was dealing with homesickness and perhaps immaturity? The language here does not allow that. He was a valued coworker, and it was an actual illness that he had suffered. Based on the note in verse 30 that he had "risked his life," some think that he had taken ill on his initial trip from Philippi to Rome and had continued on the journey while carrying the large sum of money the church had sent Paul. But if Epaphroditus had been gravely ill during his whole stay in Rome, how could he have proven himself as a faithful coworker and minister? I think it better to surmise that he had taken ill sometime after he had arrived.

However we interpret the timing, Epaphroditus had become worried that his illness was causing great anxiety to all his friends at Philippi (how they had learned of the illness remains unclear). Rather than simply sending a letter informing them of his recovery, Paul decided it would be more expedient to have Epaphroditus return home. However, Paul wanted the Philippians to know this was *his* decision (not Epaphroditus'). Paul considered Epaphroditus' emotional distress a sign of his maturity, not of immaturity—a reflection of his deep love and faithfulness.

In verse 27 Paul clarifies what had actually taken place: "Indeed he was ill, and almost died." This explains the extreme anxiety that both the Philippians and Epaphroditus felt. When a loved one is near death we naturally want continuous updates and tend to worry incessantly until we learn of their full recovery. So Paul wanted to alleviate this two-sided worry. Also, in verse 30 Paul adds "almost died for the work of Christ," thereby linking this with Jesus, who was "obedient to the point of death" (2:8). This connection would have made Epaphroditus' illness a "fellowship in [Christ's] suffering" (3:10) and thus an example of Christlike perseverance.

In mercy God intervened and spared Epaphroditus. Just as we don't know the details of his illness, we don't know how the recovery took place—through medicine or miracle or both—but judging from 2:27 God was clearly behind it. Moreover, it was a twofold mercy—on Epaphroditus, who was healed, and on Paul, who was spared deep sorrow at the death of a close friend.

Interestingly, Paul had earlier expressed his personal preference for the mercy of death so that he could be with Christ (1:21, 23). Depending on the circumstances, both living and dying can be received as gifts of divine mercy. By granting Epaphroditus a longer life on earth, God had extended his ministry and brought happiness to those who wanted to enjoy his presence with them for a while longer (as Paul admitted about himself in 1:24). His recovery was evidence of the mercy of God at work on behalf of those who loved Epaphroditus and those who would be helped spiritually through his ongoing ministry among them.

Paul considered himself one of those friends who wanted Epaphroditus around for the near future, so he recognized God's mercy on himself as well. By sparing Epaphroditus' life God had spared Paul "sorrow upon sorrow." This is a great example for us today, for I remember thinking at one time that Christians should never express sorrow at the death of a believing loved one—because death means they are with the Lord, which is a happy thing, right? I failed to realize the true tension, for death is described in 1 Corinthians 15:26 as "the last enemy to be destroyed." It is not our friend. Jesus was filled with anger that his friend Lazarus had to die (John 11:33, 38),[3] and we all naturally feel deep sorrow that we will never see our loved one again on this earth. Paul would have followed Jewish practice and beat his breast, crying his eyes out at the loss of his friend. When a believing loved one dies we are filled with conflicting emotions—sorrow that we will never see them again in this world along with joy that their suffering is over and they are with the Lord.

---

3. Most translations have Jesus "deeply moved in spirit," but the Greek word *embrimaomai* means "filled with anger" and describes Jesus' anger at the death that had claimed his friend.

HOPE FOR THE PHILIPPIANS' SAKE (2:28–30)

Paul has been discussing the reasons for returning Epaphroditus to Philippi—from his own perspective as well as from Epaphroditus' point of view. Now he considers the perspective of the Philippians themselves. Paul says he is "all the more eager to send him" when he considers the impact that the news of Epaphroditus' illness must have had on his friends back home.

The reasons—joy and honor (2:28–29)

The Philippians' anxiety is indicated in the first reason given: that they might "see him again" and "be glad." Clearly the entire church cared deeply about Epaphroditus and needed not just to hear about his recovery but to see it for themselves. "All the more eager" can also mean "as quickly as possible," indicating that Epaphroditus had only recently recovered and that Paul did not want to wait (due to the Philippians' anxiety over their friend, as well as to Epaphroditus's anxiousness to relieve their concerns).

The second reason for sending him back, Paul says, is that "I may have less anxiety." Paul had seen Epaphroditus's distress and knew of the deep concern of the Philippians, and this had led to his own increasing worries. So there were three parties feeling anxious—Epaphroditus, the Philippians, and Paul—and all would be relieved by the simple solution of Epaphroditus returning home. Philippi provides a terrific example for us of a community that has become a family. The love expressed at all three levels is wondrous to behold, and we all could wish this would describe our own churches as well.

In verse 29, Paul asks that the Philippians not just "welcome him in the Lord with great joy" but also give Epaphroditus the honor and esteem he so richly deserved. There may have been some in Philippi who would conclude from his return that he had failed in his mission, so Paul wanted not just to dispel such mistaken notions but to ask for the opposite—that they "honor people like him." Paul expresses not only great joy that God has spared Epaphroditus and brought him home healthy, but also great respect and appreciation for his successful work for the Lord. Designating him coworker, Christian soldier, and apostle— all roles he had fulfilled with distinction—Paul makes clear that Epaphroditus deserves the honor that all such Christian leaders should receive. In 1 Timothy 5:17 Paul says that elders who do well are "worthy of double honor," and he is making a similar point here.

So there are two things Paul wanted the Philippians to do when Epaphroditus arrived home: first, greet him "in the Lord" with great joy, meaning not just human happiness that he was well and had come home, but spiritual joy for all God had done through him; and second, render him the public honor and esteem he so richly deserved. This meant recognizing, perhaps in a ceremony, the success of his ministry in Rome. Paul indicates he would like this recognition to be extended to all ministers (v. 29)—an important point for churches today. There should be regular ceremonies, banquets, and other public forums in which the leaders God has given the church as his grace-gift (Eph 4:8, 11) are honored in some meaningful way for the successful ministries they have provided.

His example—risked his life (2:30)

Paul now spells out the extent of Epaphroditus's sacrificial service. He had "almost died" and had "risked his life" to fulfill his commission from the Philippians for the Lord's work. The emphasis here is on the fact that he had suffered all this "for the work of Christ." Paul uses the same term (Greek: *ergon*; "work") in 1:22 to describe his own ministry as a "fruitful labor" for Christ. Note the opposites: Epaphroditus was willing to lose his life for the work of the gospel, while Paul was willing to live for the sake of that same work. The one contemplated death, the other life, but their goal was the same—to enhance Christ's work. These men had the same priority: to spend their lives from beginning to end glorifying Christ and spreading his gospel to the lost.

It is difficult to know for certain what "risked his life" means. It could be a euphemism intended to restate the previous "almost died," in the sense that Epaphroditus literally risked death for the cause of Christ. Some think it must imply more—perhaps referring to the dangers of travel on the roads from Philippi to Rome. However, that is rather speculative, and the euphemistic meaning is more likely. This generous servant freely surrendered himself to his ministry even to the point of death, again a reminder of Christ's self-sacrifice in 2:8.

Paul's final point in this section stresses the involvement of the whole church of Philippi in Epaphroditus' sacrificial ministry. This was not a rebuke, but a commendation. Epaphroditus was discharging the "apostolic" (2:25) duty assigned to him on behalf of his church. The members of the congregation no doubt all wished they could have been helping Paul in Rome ("the help you yourselves could not give me"), but that was not feasible, so they had sent Epaphroditus as their personal representative to do that work (giving Paul both monetary and ministerial help). Paul was filled with gratitude not only to Epaphroditus but to the Philippian church that had sent him. Here the church itself is presented as a model of servanthood. This is a wonderful picture of a mission-minded congregation, of believers who consider every gift they send to actually be a part of themselves working for the Lord.

————

Against initial appearances this section of the letter is neither mundane nor relatively unimportant. These two men, Timothy and Epaphroditus, have become important models for all of us of true Christian leaders and mature followers of Christ. Timothy is a paradigm of the loving servant who forgets all about himself and his own desires in order to sacrificially and wholeheartedly serve the Lord and the Lord's people. He shows us how to live a Christ-filled life in which our own agenda is placed on the back burner while we give ourselves wholly to meet the needs of those to whom God has sent us. Epaphroditus is a paradigm of the dedicated, mature Christian who accepts hardship and unflinchingly perseveres to the very point of death in order to serve God and the gospel ministry. He shows us how to soldier on and find victory in Christ through even the most severe difficulties.

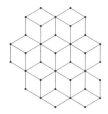

A NEW CRISIS: THE JUDAIZERS
ARRIVE IN PHILIPPI
(3:1–11)

The beginning of Philippians 3 presents the most difficult interpretive issue in this letter. The opening phrase in Greek, *to loipon*, is rendered "further" in the NIV but also could be translated "finally" (as in the ESV, KJV, NASB, and NRSV). This sounds like the intended conclusion of the letter, but verse 2 changes tack completely and introduces another opponent, a group of evildoers Paul calls "the dogs." Due to the abrupt change in focus, some interpreters believe this to be a fragment of another letter inserted into the Philippian letter at this point. This is possible; in fact, if we skip over 3:2-21, the letter reads very well. It is much smoother to move from "rejoice in the Lord" (3:1) to the gentle admonitions of chapter 4 than to the curses against the heretics of chapter 3. However, two other lines of interpretation make such a hypothesis unnecessary.

First, we must take a closer look at the identity of the opponents in chapter 3. Many interpreters see them as the internal antagonists of 1:15-18 or the external persecutors of 1:27-30. Either is possible, though the language of chapter 3 would favor the former, since these individuals seem to be false teachers coming from *within* the Christian movement, while the persecutors of 1:27–30 are the non-Christians of Philippi. However, there is a problem in linking the rivals of 1:15–18 and those of chapter 3: In 1:18 Paul rejoices in that very group who seems to have been opposing his ministry, because "whether from false motives or true, Christ is preached." This is not what we find with the heretics of chapter 3, who did not preach Christ, but rather were "enemies of the cross of Christ" who were destined for destruction (3:18–19). So I believe that chapter 3 gives us a third group of opponents at Philippi, different from both the rival preachers of the gospel in 1:18–20 and the pagan persecutors of 1:27–30. It is likely that they were **Judaizers**—that is, Jewish Christians who demanded adherence to the law of Moses (the **Torah**) as a purported requirement for Christian salvation (similar to the "circumcision group" Paul mentions in Galatians 2:12).

Building on this view of the opponents' identity, a second line of interpretation becomes available with respect to the transition from 3:1 to 3:2. I believe that these Judaizers had recently arrived in Philippi and had started making inroads into the church there, so that Paul had just received word of their influence at this point in composing his letter. Immediately he stopped writing his conclusion and switched to a diatribe against his enemies of the recent past.[1] To me this makes better sense of the change in tone between verse 1 and verse 2. This then introduces a third problem area Paul needed to address in the letter—a Judaizing false teaching (3:1–4:1), following the earlier discussions of persecution (1:27–30) and dissension (2:1–18). Paul proceeds to argue against these dangerous heretics based on themes he had taught the Philippians on a previous occasion ("the same things to you again," 3:1), presenting himself as a further paradigm for the believers ("follow my example," v. 17) in addition to the models he describes in chapter 2 (Christ, Timothy, and Epaphroditus).

---

1. Galatians was written about twelve years earlier, in AD 49.

PAUL WARNS ABOUT THE JUDAIZING
FALSE TEACHERS (3:1-3)

The Need to Rejoice (3:1a)

At this point Paul is penning an intended conclusion to his letter. He believed the Philippians would heed his admonition and work out the problem of dissension, leading to a deep-seated joy at the Lord's work among them. The Greek verb translated "rejoice" is present tense, so Paul is asking for an ongoing sense of joy in the Lord. God was in charge and would infuse the believers with spiritual strength to bring peace and unity to their church and to turn the pressure from the pagans (1:27-30) into victory in Christ.

The command to rejoice has come twice before in the letter, in 1:18 and 2:17-18, both times in response to the advance of the gospel amid opposition and hardship. Joy is especially meaningful for Christians in adverse circumstances, for it then must center entirely "in the Lord," not in the circumstances themselves. In Philippians 1:18 Paul could rejoice even though the preaching of his rivals included scurrilous attacks against him, and in 2:17-18 he experienced joy even while facing the possibility that he would soon be executed. The point for us is that God's presence turns even the most troublesome situation into an occasion for joy, because we know that our loving Father will not just get us through the valley of the shadow of death (Ps 23:4) but will bring victory out of defeat. So this command was meant to sum up Paul's earlier remarks and conclude the letter on a note of joy.

The Safeguard and Warning (3:1b-2)

At this point in writing the letter, Paul probably received word that his old opponents from the Jerusalem council (Acts 15) had arrived in Philippi and were gaining influence there. Perhaps he had just finished his opening words—"Further, my brothers and sisters, rejoice in the Lord"—when the message came. Paul proceeds by indicating why he is making such a sudden departure from his intended ending. He wants his readers to know it is not difficult for him to write "the same things." It is difficult to ascertain what this refers to, as there is nothing in chapter 3 that seems to repeat material from the first two chapters. Some interpreters think this statement involves his call to rejoice in 3:1a, but that doesn't seem to relate well to the presence of the heretics, the subject of chapter 3. Others suggest that the admonitions about the heretics hark back to a previous teaching the Philippians had received; this scenario makes more sense, accounting for 3:1b as Paul's segue into the topic. He would have been telling his readers once again what they had previously been taught—which was all the more critical now that the false teachers had arrived in their city.

Note the contrast: "to me" it is not "irksome" or burdensome to say what needs to be said, but "for you" it is a "safeguard" (that is, "for your safety"). The Philippian believers were in grave danger from these heretics and needed a serious warning, lest they fall prey to them (as the Galatians had done). The Greek word for "safeguard" (*asphales*) also speaks of spiritual stability, so Paul is indicating that these warnings were needed in order to stabilize the congregation and avert the kind of theological chaos that could result from following the Judaizers' heresy. The admonition in verse 2 takes the form of three straight commands, all using the Greek verb *blepete* ("watch out") and each followed by a description of these false teachers: "Watch out for those dogs, watch out for those evildoers, watch out for those mutilators of the flesh."

Before getting into the details, we need to better understand who these heretics were. There is general agreement that they were Judaizers, belonging to a movement of Jewish Christ-followers who wanted to make all Christians followers and practitioners of Judaism. This movement began in reaction to the universal gospel proclaimed first by Peter (after the conversion of Cornelius in Acts 11) and then by Paul. At first nearly everyone agreed with Peter's defense (Acts 11:4-17) of the coming of the Spirit upon the Gentile God-fearer Cornelius, recognizing that "even to Gentiles God has granted repentance that leads to life" (Acts 11:18). Very quickly, however, a group had begun to dispute this, most of them former Pharisees and all of them completely committed to the ongoing necessity of Torah-observance and circumcision—not just for Jewish converts to Christianity, but for Gentile Christians as well.[2] The Judaizers (a designation often used by later interpreters but not during Paul's time) sent emissaries to the Gentile churches that Paul and Barnabas had established on the first missionary journey, but they were opposed by Paul in his Galatian letter and defeated at the council of Jerusalem in Acts 15. Still, they continued to reject that decision and to travel around to Gentile churches, telling all believers that they had to live as Jews in order to be Christians. In Galatians Paul says the Judaizers proclaimed "a different gospel" and that they were "under God's curse" (Gal 1:6, 8).

Paul responds in the same way here in Philippians. The three epithets in 3:2 are all drawn from Jewish metaphors. Dogs were unclean animals that were viewed negatively, especially in that packs of wild dogs roamed the countryside and were dangerous nuisances. Since dogs were particularly noted for eating garbage, the Jews used "dogs" as an epithet for Gentiles who failed to follow the Jewish dietary laws and were thereby "unclean." Paul is turning that metaphor on its head, saying that these false Jewish "Christians" were the truly impure dogs who stood outside the covenant of God.

---

2. The nature of the Judaizing group remains a topic of debate. Some commentators acknowledge that the Judaizers could have included Gentile believers who already had converted to Judaism (i.e., they had been circumcised) and were trying to persuade other Gentiles to follow the same path. It appears that the Judaizers sincerely believed that Gentiles must join the ethnic people of Israel in order to follow Jesus faithfully.

The same reversal of use applies to "evildoers." From the perspective of the Jewish people, the Gentiles rejected God and his Torah and so were "those who do evil" (Pss 6:8; 14:4; 36:12; 94:4). Paul's point here is that true evil no longer consisted of failing to keep the law, but rather involved doing that which undermined the gospel of Christ—a description now embodied by these false teachers. Paul was turning the importance of "works" against them; they were doing not the works of God but evil works. These Judaizers had a mission that was the direct opposite of Paul's, for they went forth spreading the "gospel" of Torah observance, not the gospel of Christ and the cross. Their stance constituted true heresy, since they were replacing the cross with the Torah.

This is exactly what Paul means by "mutilators of the flesh." He is using the imagery of circumcision—the primary Jewish sign of membership in God's covenant—against these pro-circumcision teachers. The Greek word for circumcision is *peritomē*, and the word for mutilation is *katatomē*. Since the Judaizers had replaced the cross with circumcision as the means of salvation, they had, in Paul's view, changed the rite of circumcision into an act of mutilation, for their covenant ceremony actually "cut off" people from salvation. This is the most serious of Paul's charges against these opponents, for circumcision is at the heart of the Jewish conception of covenant, encompassing the whole idea of Torah-observance and covenant faithfulness. In effect, those who promoted circumcision rejected the new covenant established by Christ through the cross; in trying to return to the old covenant, they ended up with no covenant at all. Such people, Paul insisted, were entirely cut off from God and from his grace and mercy in Christ.

The Description of True vs. False Believers (3:3)

Still continuing his contrast between true circumcision and the Judaizers' mutilation, Paul asserts, "For it is we who are the circumcision"—referring to Christians as the real people of God.

The people of Israel could no longer be called "the circumcision," for they had rejected their Messiah, the Son of God, and as a result no longer had the Spirit. As in Romans 2:29, "a person is a Jew who is one inwardly, and circumcision is circumcision of the heart by the Spirit, not by the written code." It is the heart, not external appearance, that determines the true Israel, and that now consists entirely of Christ-followers. Jews and Gentiles alike who follow Christ are joint members of God's family, not by ancestral pedigree or physical circumcision as the covenant sign but via heart-belief by way of the cross.

Paul follows this up with three clauses that define the new Israel, the people of the new covenant. It is clear that human status, inheritance, and achievement avail nothing, and that salvation comes entirely via the unmerited grace and mercy of God. First, we "serve God by his Spirit," with the Greek verb *latreuō* carrying a double meaning here of "serve" and "worship." While some versions translate *latreuō* as "worship" (KJV, ESV, LEB, NASB, NET, NLT, and NRSV), the **Septuagint** (the Greek translation of the Old Testament) normally uses it for Levitical service in the temple, so "service" (NIV, HCSB) is probably better here. However, such service included worship "in Spirit and in truth" (John 4:23–24), and Paul had both concepts in view. The Judaizers claimed they served God by keeping the Torah, but they were doing so in a fleshly way, without the empowerment of the Holy Spirit. Only in coming to God by faith in Christ (Eph 2:8, 9) can one receive the Spirit (Rom 8:14–17) and be sealed by the Spirit (Eph 1:13–14; 4:30).

Second, we "boast in Christ Jesus," building on Philippians 1:26, 2:16, where Paul's point is that true boasting is not in the self or in human achievement but in Christ and the things of Christ. The Judaizers were entirely fleshly, and their pride was in law-observance rather than in Christ. In 1 Corinthians 1:31 and 2 Corinthians 10:17, Paul quotes Jeremiah 9:24, "Let the one who boasts boast in the Lord." There is a place for Christian pride, but it must never be centered on self—only on Christ and what he has achieved. The Judaizers could boast in the works of the law and in their own ritual purity, but those could never be enough. The only way anyone can be right with God is through the work of Christ on the cross—the only appropriate grounds for boasting and pride.

Third, we "put no confidence in the flesh," and that includes circumcision. This is the negative side of "boasting in Christ," a no-flesh-but-Christ confidence and boasting. This is exactly how Paul defines salvation in Ephesians 2:8–9—by grace, not by works, "so that no one can boast." The Judaizers had an opposite locus of salvation, in effect claiming it to be by works and not by grace. There is a double meaning for "flesh" here, referring, first, to the fleshly rite of circumcision and, second, to the fleshly descent of covenant, centering on national identity and ancestral heritage (according to the Judaizers). Right relationship with God is spiritual and of the Spirit, centered in the atoning sacrifice of Christ and not in ceremony or ancestry.

The message of Philippians 3:1–3 is clear: Any attempt to place our confidence in our earthly relationships or human achievements is doomed to fail. All non-Christian religions, including that of the Judaizers here, are in the end nothing more that pride-filled attempts to earn our own salvation by our works. We can become a part of the new Israel, the true people of God, only when our boasting is centered in Christ and our action involves faith in him and his work on the cross. The unmerited grace of God is the basis of our salvation. We can purchase nothing; rather, we have been purchased by Christ for God.

PAUL REFLECTS ON THE REASONS FOR HIS CONFIDENCE IN HIS PAST PEDIGREE (3:4–6)

Paul now compares his right to speak with that of his opponents. The Judaizers claimed they had a greater right to be heard, for in their eyes Paul was a false apostle who was subverting the law.

So Paul demonstrates here that his pedigree was much stronger than theirs, giving him a greater right to be heard. Furthermore, he presents his own life as a fourth paradigm or model to be followed (vv. 4–14 develop this), after those of Christ (2:5–11), Timothy (2:19–24), and Epaphroditus (2:25–30). Paul's point is that the Philippians should follow his example rather than that of the Judaizers, and in 3:4–11 he offers his personal testimony to illustrate the meaning of "no confidence in the flesh." He could speak on the subject as an insider, having spent much of his life as a Jewish leader with a reputation centered on his fleshly pedigree. Here in verses 4–6 he develops the extent of his pedigree, showing that in the fleshly sense he had more authority to instruct the Philippians than the Judaizers did. Then in verses 7–11 Paul goes on to say unequivocally that nothing in this fleshly pedigree suffices. Indeed, it can only be counted as loss so that he can "boast in Christ."

The Reasons for His Confidence (3:4)

Paul begins with the superiority of his personal reasons for confidence, over against the claims of the Judaizers. He is arguing on the level of his opponents; they have challenged him on the basis of Torah, so Paul is responding at the level of those who claim expertise in Torah and who represent a high Jewish pedigree. He, far more than they, has "reasons for such confidence" in the flesh. Within the Jewish hierarchy, very few people reached a higher status than Paul had achieved. Starting around the age of thirteen, he had trained under the leading rabbi of his day (see below on 3:5b–6), eventually becoming an expert in the interpretation of the Torah. As a young man, Paul had been a leader in the Jewish movement against Christianity and had been given authority to expand the persecution to Jewish communities outside Palestine. So his pedigree was much higher than that of the Judaizers. He goes on to list seven advantages he possessed over them, the first four from his inherited birthright and the last three his personal achievements.

HIS PRIVILEGED INHERITED POSITION (3:5A)

1. Circumcised on the eighth day—This tells the reader that Paul was legitimately Jewish from birth (eighth-day circumcision was the expected covenant rite; Gen 17:12; Lev 12:3). According to the fleshly way of thinking, this fact made him superior to Gentile converts to Judaism (proselytes), who likely had not been circumcised until adulthood.

2. Of the people of Israel—This is similar to the first point and centers on racial privileges; the proselytes were ethnically non-Jewish, while Paul had always been completely Jewish. By virtue of his birth to Jewish parents, he possessed all the status and privileges of the covenant people, as enumerated in Romans 9:4–5: "adoption to sonship, the divine glory, the covenants, the receiving of the law, the temple worship, and the promises."

3. Of the tribe of Benjamin—After the presumed death of Joseph, Benjamin had become Jacob's favorite son (Gen 42:38). The tribe that descended from Benjamin was the origin of Israel's first king, Saul (1 Sam 9:1–2), the namesake of Saul/Paul. This tribe had joined with Judah in remaining faithful to the house of David when the others had rebelled, and its territory included the city of Jerusalem (Judg 1:21). Paul was justly proud of his tribal heritage (compare Rom 11:1).

4. A Hebrew of Hebrews—This may have implied that Paul's family spoke Aramaic at home and was especially careful to maintain the dietary laws and other Jewish customs even though they lived in Tarsus, outside the Jewish homeland. In other words, Paul's family was among those who adamantly refused to be adopt a Greco-Roman lifestyle.

His Personal Achievements (3:5b-6)

1. In regard to the law, a Pharisee—Since his early adolescence, Paul had trained under the rabbi Gamaliel, grandson of the renowned rabbi Hillel (Acts 5:34; 22:3) and a leader among the Pharisees. This Jewish party had evolved from the Hasidim, devout Jews who had helped lead the Maccabean revolt (167-160 bc) against the **Hellenistic** rulers of Judea and had developed the oral Torah. Paul would have grown up obeying these extra laws, along with the written Torah. Speaking in Acts, Paul describes the Pharisees as the "strictest sect" among the Jews (Acts 26:5); by calling himself a Pharisee here in Philippians, he is reminding his readers that he had practiced a particularly stringent form of Judaism (Gal 1:14) compared to his opponents. Paul's point is that *he* was the one who had authority to teach on Jewish legal matters.

2. As for zeal, persecuting the church—In Galatians, Paul acknowledges how zealously he had persecuted the Christians (Gal 1:13-14). He was present at the stoning of Stephen, the first martyr of the early church (Acts 7:58), and he even obtained letters of commendation from the Sanhedrin (the Jewish ruling council) authorizing him to initiate persecution in areas beyond Palestine (Acts 9:1-2). The Jews believed that, so long as there was blasphemy in the land, the Messiah would not come. Therefore, in helping to eradicate the Christian movement—participating even in the execution of several believers (Acts 26:10)— Paul had thought he was removing obstacles to the coming of God's kingdom. He later came to believe that his persecution of the church had been the worst of his offenses (1 Cor 15:9; 1 Tim 1:15). Here in Philippians, he cites his zealous activity against the church to show he had

both knowledge and experience on matters of Torah and on Jewish-Christian issues.

3. As for righteousness based on the law, faultless—The Pharisees believed that righteousness was determined by the extent to which one kept the law (both the written and the oral Torah), and in that endeavor Paul had been exceptionally faithful. He was not, of course, claiming perfection, but he had been incredibly scrupulous in observing the details of the law's requirements. Paul spells out the true weakness of this approach in Romans 7; here, his point is that he knew what he was talking about on legal issues. Again, if anyone were qualified to speak with authority on matters of Torah, it would have been Paul, not the Judaizers.

PAUL TURNS TO THE GREATER VALUE OF HIS PRESENT STATUS BEFORE GOD (3:7-11)

Paul asserts his credentials (vv. 4-6) for the sake of argument against the Judaizers. One can never rely on family pedigree or personal achievements. Any "gain" from such a background is theoretical rather than actual, for what matters is not past accolades but a relationship with Christ in the present. In fact, as Paul goes on to explain in verses 7-11, the criteria that raise one's reputation in the world are actually liabilities with God, having no value in an eternal sense.

ALL PAST GAINS ARE PRESENT LOSS (3:7)

To emphasize the powerful turnaround Paul experienced, he presents the material in verses 7-9a in a **chiastic** order:

> A whatever were gains
>> B I now consider loss for the sake of Christ
>> B′ I consider everything a loss because of the surpassing worth of knowing Christ
> A′ that I might gain Christ and be found in him

Paul writes these lines as a heavenly accountant, presenting a ledger for developing true gain out of illusory earthly gains. Here the gain-loss account has three columns: earthly gains, everything counted as loss, and true gain. Note that the earthly gains are plural and contain Paul's past achievements from verses 4-6, as well as his current achievements that come into view in verse 8 (see below). But the loss column is singular; here, the human gains are not worthy of being listed separately. Taken together, Paul considers them all a loss, for only Christ and the things linked to him have eternal value. The true goal of life is not legal righteousness by keeping human regulations (even those of the Torah) but spiritual righteousness that leads to eternal life.

The opening phrase, "whatever were gains to me," sums up all seven advantages from verses 4-6, as well as anything else Paul could have listed along with them. Yet at the same time it goes beyond them to include anything at all that could have been viewed as an advantage for Paul. The seven are representative of anything he could have listed as profitable, anything that could have given him "confidence in the flesh" (v. 4). But now that Paul is "in Christ" he has a new perspective—the mindset of Christ (2:5)—that causes him to reconsider his priorities. In light of Christ, all these gains have fallen into a single category, that of "loss." Indeed, that which is advantageous from an earthly perspective becomes a liability "because of Christ," the focal point of Paul's new heavenly perspective. When the world sets the agenda these factors are hugely advantageous, but when Christ is in first place the polar opposite is true, and we realize how great a disadvantage they really are. This becomes a kind of renunciation formula, as we renounce what used to control our lives. Note that this demands an act of the mind and will as we come to "consider" our former advantages as loss. For us, these gain-loss items would be anything that amounts to earthly profit, including our ethnic heritage, economic birthright, educational credentials, workplace achievements, etc. Christ and Christ alone must be on the throne of our lives.

THE SURPASSING VALUE OF KNOWING CHRIST (3:8–9)

Everything loss to know Christ (3:8a)

With the phrase "what is more," Paul expands the horizons of this passage. The gain-loss antithesis in verse 7 was centered on past advantages. Paul now turns to the present setting and universalizes the list. For Paul the past things would have been his Jewish pedigree and achievements, and the "everything" of verse 8 would have included all the good he had done in his Christian ministry as well. The point is that knowing Christ had taken precedence even over his ministry objectives. Having been a Christian leader myself for more than fifty years, I know how easily even mission and ministry objectives can lead to coldness of heart, how busy-ness in church work can replace time with the Lord, and how ideas of worldly success and material possessions can replace love for the Lord and his people. There are countless well-known Christian speakers who charge a small fortune to address a church gathering. I wouldn't want to face the Lord after turning ministry into a get-rich-quick scheme!

Paul further expands the scope in verse 8 by intensifying the meaning of "because of Christ" from verse 7. Now it is "the surpassing worth of knowing Christ Jesus my Lord." This clause continues the accounting imagery, emphasizing that the gain to be had in Christ is vastly superior to any earthly gain one could imagine. If we compare Christ with mere money or fame there is no contest; Christ wins hands down. Moreover, the advantage comes from "knowing Christ," combining intellectual and experiential knowledge. In comparison with knowing Jesus there is zero profit in any earthly attainment or possession. To get to know Jesus personally is a lifelong endeavor, similar to marriage and family: You never exhaust the joy of being drawn closer and closer together as day builds upon day and year upon year.

Moreover, the Greek text highlights coming to know "Christ Jesus as my Lord." In addition to knowing him as my friend and brother, I also learn to trust him as sovereign Lord over every part of my life, knowing he loves me and has control over every aspect of my existence. I come to understand the depths of his love—that even while I was a sinner and wanted nothing to do with him, he died for me (Rom 5:8; Gal 2:20). This God of very God (Phil 2:6) surrendered his life on the cross (2:7-8) so that I could live. This God of very God was raised and exalted above his creation in order to guide and direct my life. As every Christian can confess, he is not just "*a* Lord" but "*my* Lord," watching over me so that every single thing that happens will work together for my good (Rom 8:28). How can anything the world has to offer compare with this!

Everything garbage to gain Christ (3:8b–9a)

For the sake of Christ Jesus my Lord, Paul asserts, "I have lost all things." For emphasis, he now switches from nouns ("loss," "gains") to verbs ("I have lost ... that I might gain"). The force is active, denoting something that takes great effort—not just to "consider" these gains as loss (as in v. 7), but to actually "suffer loss" on Christ's behalf in order to gain that which is infinitely superior. Moreover, it is not enough to consider *all* earthly gains to be "loss." Everything that produces human advantage must be cast out as loss. We are to consider all such things as "garbage," worthy only for the trash heap.

Paul uses a surprisingly strong Greek word (*skybala*) to indicate the kind of rubbish or garbage thrown out for the wild dogs to consume, or even dung or excrement that goes down the toilet. This is the strongest possible term for something that has become too vile even to keep in the house; it might be fit for the "dogs" of verse 2, but it is not at all appropriate for a child of God. Since the Judaizers observed a fleshly religion, they deserved these putrid, fleshly "gains," for they would never know Christ so long as they persisted in their worldly pursuits. Believers, however, recognize such pursuits as refuse and so have nothing to do with them. If more of us would take this perspective, revival would come to the church and the world would be changed.

When such worldly goals have been cast out of our lives, we are in a position to "gain Christ and be found in him." This clause introduces the "true gain" stage of the accounting metaphor Paul develops throughout this passage, but we cannot reach this stage in our lives without first adopting the "everything counted as loss/garbage" perspective. So long as the world dictates the goals we seek, we cannot truly know Christ. As Jesus said in the Sermon on the Mount, "No one can serve two masters ... God and money" (Matt 6:24). Too many believers want both worlds, but Jesus and Paul say that is impossible; we cannot have both Christ *and* the world, for to have the latter cancels out the former. A true believer cannot tithe her life—that is, give ten percent to Christ and keep the rest for herself. Such a quasi-Christian is in grave danger of facing Jesus' scathing rebuke in Matthew 7:23: "I never knew you. Away from me, you evildoers!"

On the other hand, the one who truly counts everything loss for the sake of Christ will truly and completely "gain Christ and be found in him." There is an "already but not yet" aspect to being "found in him," dealing with both present and future salvation. The present aspect is defined in two ways: first by Romans 3:24, which says we are "justified," declared "right" with God; and then by Romans 8:14–17, which describes the Spirit bringing about our "adoption to sonship," when we become members of God's family. Here in Philippians 3, these realities are implied by the phrase "in him" (v. 9a), as believers are now "in Christ"—united with him and made members of his body.

The "not yet" aspect involves what still awaits the believer, and it is clearly part of Paul's thrust in these verses. There is a great deal of emphasis in Philippians on the "day of Christ" (1:6, 10; 2:16; see also 3:11, 14, 21). The point here is the finalization of our new status at the **eschaton** (end of the present age), the beginning of our heavenly reign. In this verse (3:9a) our present status in Christ and our future life with him come together. We are presently "found in him," yet we await our future and final place in heaven. Our present total surrender and dependence on him alone will fill our future reality with meaning and content. This is the biblical doctrine of treasures in heaven (Matt 6:19–21): We will take with us into eternity all that we have done for Christ, for the church, and for others (our gains) and will forever suffer the loss of those earthly possessions, pursuits, and concerns we should have considered loss all along.

The true gain—righteousness based on faith (3:9b)

Paul goes on to discuss his "gain" from knowing Christ in the language of "righteousness." In the rest of verse 9, he actually presents two kinds of righteousness that are in sharp contrast to one another—self-righteousness vs. a Christ-centered righteousness. The former is expressed negatively: Paul desires to be found "not having a righteousness of my own that comes from the law." There is quite a debate today over this statement. Followers of the so-called "New Perspective on Paul"[3] argue that this is not a legalistic righteousness achieved by good deeds; rather, it is an ethnic-oriented righteousness associated with being an observant Jew. In this view, Paul's specific argument here is not against obeying the law as a means of earning righteousness.[4] Instead, says the New Perspective, Paul is arguing against using the law as

---

3. See E. P. Sanders, *Paul, the Law, and the Jewish People* (Philadelphia: Fortress Press, 1985).

4. To be clear, scholars who follow the New Perspective readily acknowledge that Paul would have opposed this suggestion. However, in their view, the Jewish law did not function in Paul's time as a means of earning righteousness; consequently, they say, there was no reason for Paul to argue against such a view.

a boundary marker that would require Gentiles to become Jews in order to join the body of Christ.

While interesting, this does not fit the language here. Paul is responding to the Judaizers and their view that righteousness was achieved by the works of the law, but that still entailed a self-righteousness that came via good deeds. A righteousness attained through the law is inadequate because Christ has fulfilled the law (Matt 5:17-20; Rom 10:4), and only that which comes through Christ and the cross can be true righteousness. There can be nothing of self in true righteousness; it is never "my own" but is always and entirely the gift of God through Christ's atoning work on the cross (Gal 2:20; Eph 2:8-9).

So the true basis of being "found in him" is "through faith in Christ—that righteousness that comes from God on the basis of faith." This new righteousness through Christ is not moral or legal but relational. It is nothing that we have earned through righteous behavior but is based entirely on the reconciling work of Christ. It is a gift rather than an achievement, and this gift is related to our new status—to the reality that we are "in Christ" and members of his body, the church. The "righteousness that comes from God" refers to the new status that comes to us on the basis of our justification; God has rendered a verdict and declared us both innocent and in right relationship with himself on the basis of the redemptive work of Christ.

With this in mind, it seems viable that the Greek phrase *pisteōs Christou* might here mean not "faith in Christ" but "the faithfulness of Christ," reflecting not our own salvific faith but Christ's obedience to his calling to die on the cross and bring salvation to us. However, while this would fit the context, Paul's other uses of this phrase (Gal 2:16; 3:22; Rom 3:22, 26) make it more likely that he is speaking of our faith in Jesus rather than of his faithful actions. While Paul could be referring to Christ's faithfulness in the first clause and our faith in Christ in the second ("on the basis of faith"), it is more likely that both clauses denote the same kind of faith—namely, our faith in Christ that leads God to give us new status as members of Christ's body. Everything we have and are has come to us on the basis of our faith-response to God's free gift of salvation, and our present and future status as members of the kingdom community is the direct result.

The True Goal—to Know Christ (3:10-11)

Paul now unpacks what he means by knowing Christ (v. 8). His remarks fall into three categories: the content of knowing him, the means by which knowing him is possible, and the goal of knowing him. Once again, this knowledge is experiential as well as intellectual. We have a new relationship with Christ, and these are the aspects of that new personal connection.

The content—to know Christ, his resurrection, and his sufferings (3:10a)

This first category includes three textual elements. The verb phrase "to know him" is an infinitive of purpose, showing God's intended result in granting us his salvation. This in a real sense describes our sanctification, a lifelong process of a deeper and deeper experience with Christ that will culminate in what Paul describes in 3:21: Our "lowly bodies" will be transformed to resemble his "glorious body." In the short lives we live, we will never exhaust the richness of that personal relationship with him. Living out the law has been replaced by knowing Christ. There is no need to keep a diary of our repeated efforts to perform good deeds that count as righteousness. The Christian life involves effort, to be sure, but it is a single, ongoing effort of coming to know Christ in greater and greater intimacy.

The next two elements—the "power of his resurrection" and the "fellowship of his sufferings"—further explain what it means to know Christ deeply. In the Greek text these elements form one idea and are inextricably linked. The "power of his resurrection" is described well in Ephesians 1:19-20: "[God's] incomparably great power ... the same as the mighty strength he exerted when he raised Christ from the dead." Several interpreters see this as denoting the power of Christ in the believer's life, but behind it is the power of God at work in us. So this is the power of the Triune Godhead that gives us new life, as we are resurrected from death at our conversion (Rom 6:3-4) and at the end of life are resurrected for eternity. This power is also at work continuously in the Christian life, enabling us to live victoriously (through the Spirit, as in Phil 3:3 above), defeat sin in our lives (Rom 6:17-18, 22-23), and stand against the cosmic powers arrayed against us (Eph 6:10-12). This is intimately connected to verse 11, which points to the final consummation of God's kingdom, when we will inherit our resurrection body (see also Phil 3:21).

To know Christ and his power also means to know "the partnership/fellowship (*koinōnia*) of his sufferings." We experience his resurrection power in the midst of experiencing his suffering. In fact, suffering brings forth power. This is connected to the doctrine of the messianic woes[5]—the belief that God had established a certain amount of suffering for his messianic community, beginning with Christ and including his followers, and that this suffering would bring his power to bear on the church and lead to the final victory at the end of the present age. These two messianic components—power and suffering—form the two sides of the same coin and are part of coming to know Christ. Here, as in 1 Peter, the theme is that suffering is the path to glory and the road to power.

For the Philippian believers the primary form of suffering had been persecution (1:27-30), which apparently was severe enough for Paul to speak of their fright and to explain the place of suffering in the Christian life: "It has been granted to you on behalf of Christ not only to believe in him, but also to suffer for him" (1:29). Yet suffering also has **eschatological** ramifications,

---

5. Reflected in Colossians 1:24, 1 Peter 4:12-13, and Revelation 6:11.

as in 3:21, where we are told that Christ at his return "will transform our lowly bodies so that they will be like his glorious body."
Through his use of the term "lowly" Paul is including the idea of
suffering and promising that we will be vindicated and repaid
for all that we endure for Christ. Christ's humiliation led to his
exaltation (2:6–11), and we will share in that scenario. I recall two
leaders of house churches in China being asked how the Chinese
church had the strength to explode in growth during the horrible
persecution from 1970 on. They looked at each other and replied
in sync: "suffering." Their suffering had given them the spiritual
power to turn severe persecution into evangelistic victory.

The key is that suffering is a "fellowship" or "participation" in
the sufferings of Christ. Suffering is a critical part of our union
with Christ, our being "in him." The more we give up for Christ,
the more we enter into—participate or take part in—who he is.
Since Christ "made himself nothing" (2:7) for us, we in turn are
to empty ourselves for him, letting go of our earthly attachments.
In Philippians 2:1 Paul notes our "fellowship (koinōnia) in the
Spirit," and that is connected to the idea here at 3:10. To participate in Christ's sufferings is to participate in the "Spirit of Christ"
(Phil 1:19; see also Acts 16:7; Rom 8:9; 1 Pet 1:11). In other words,
suffering bears a trinitarian character, as the entire Godhead
becomes involved in our lives when we participate in the messianic woes. Moreover, we share in this together with all who are in
Christ's body. The messianic community suffers with us, mourning when we mourn and rejoicing when we rejoice (Rom 12:15;
1 Cor 12:26; Heb 13:3). Suffering as believers is never meant to be
an isolated experience. We share it with Christ, with his Spirit,
and with one another.

The means—like Christ in his death (3:10b)

Paul's statement about "becoming like [Christ] in his death" is
a participial phrase modifying "to know" as well as all three
aspects of our knowing Christ. It conveys the means by which

all this new "knowledge" is made possible. Many commentators link this statement entirely with "the fellowship of his sufferings" and interpret it as a restatement of the meaning of suffering. Grammatically this is incorrect; the participial phrase modifies the infinitive ("to know") and thus all three of the related aspects. It is indeed necessary for us to die with Christ before we can be raised with him (Rom 6:3–4) and come to know him. Much of our discussion of Philippians has been based on this point, for the paradigm of Christ centers on dying to this world so we can experience his resurrection power. To be conformed to his image is to be conformed to his death. In Romans 6:6 we are told that "our old self was crucified with him so that the body ruled by sin might be done away with." Every aspect of becoming a follower of Christ is dependent on dying with him to sin and to this world. At the same time, there is a **chiasm** in verses 10–11:

> A the power of his resurrection
>> B the fellowship of his sufferings
>> B′ being conformed to his death
> A′ the resurrection from the dead

The core is the death-resurrection experience, the whole concept of receiving power through suffering. This is how we can rejoice in the midst of suffering trials (Jas 1:2; 1 Pet 1:6)—because suffering releases the power of Christ and enables us to face our hardships with a sense of Christ's and the Spirit's presence with us. We die to this world as we defeat sin, and we die further as we encounter the vagaries of this world—all of those things that bring suffering into our lives, especially evil and the activities of the Evil One and his minions as they turn the world against us. All of this makes us more like Christ, and when his power enables us to triumph over evil and the world's suffering, we become more Christlike and attain "the whole measure of the fullness of Christ" (Eph 4:13).

Finally, there also might be in this statement a hint of martyrdom; to be "like him in his death" could include losing one's life for Christ in a literal sense. This is not the primary meaning, but it might be a secondary thrust, as in Mark 8:34: "Whoever wants to be my disciple must deny themselves and take up their cross and follow me." The idea behind "take up their cross" also could connote a willingness to suffer martyrdom for Christ.

The goal—attain Christ's resurrection (3:11)

Verse 10 deals with present realities, and verse 11 turns to future promises—to the end of the present age when we receive our resurrection bodies, as in 3:21 (and 1 Cor 15:51-57; 1 Thess 4:13-18). Christ was raised from the dead as the "firstfruits" guaranteeing our own resurrection (1 Cor 15:20, 23).

The language of Philippians 3:11 is strange, beginning with "if somehow," which seems to indicate doubt. In reality, Paul had no doubt about the resurrection of God's people, for that is guaranteed by the Spirit.[6] The uncertainty relates instead to the path that each of us will take before we arrive at that point—specifically, the sufferings and difficulties that await us and the spiritual warfare we will endure on our way to that goal. There can be no doubt about the reality of the future promise, but each of us will nonetheless arrive with difficulty as we "take up [our] cross" (Mark 8:34).

The road itself is set. We are asked to live for Christ in the midst of an evil world, to be conformed to his image as we pass through the trials of this world and learn to live victoriously in him. When we die, we will immediately be in Christ's presence in our spirit and live with him in heaven (the intermediate state; 2 Cor 5:1-10) until he returns. At that time we will receive our glorified, resurrected bodies and assume our final form for eternity. So we have the power of his resurrection for the present and are guaranteed resurrection from the dead in our future. The cross dominates our present, and Christ's resurrection will consume

---

6. Seen as an "inheritance" in Ephesians 1:13, 14; 4:30; see also 1 Corinthians 15:20; 2 Corinthians 5:1.

our future. This is why we have a "living hope" (1 Pet 1:3) in our final inheritance.

———

While we want to be tolerant of Christians from different theological persuasions, there are certain cardinal beliefs that are nonnegotiable. These are made clear in Scripture: the Trinity, the deity of Christ, substitutionary atonement, etc. One of these is the doctrine of salvation by grace alone through Christ's atoning sacrifice on the cross. The Judaizers rejected this and made salvation dependent on circumcision and Torah-observance. When we face such heresies, we are called to respond with the gospel of Christ and his cross, as Paul does here in Philippians 3.

However, the idea of counting everything loss and casting it out as garbage is difficult in our modern world. How far is the average Christian to take this? Are we to refuse to work hard at our jobs or to seek profit to take care of our families? Are *all* material possessions evil and meant to be rejected? Medieval monks adopted such an extreme approach, but the Christians of the first century—including Paul—did not take things that far. The key is to consider our earthly career or job a ministry to which Christ has called us. Teachers, engineers, and medical people are called to their work just as pastors and missionaries are called. God has placed us where we are, and he wants us to glorify him where we are, so we become the best truck drivers or staff assistants we can be. Our primary goal is to magnify Christ where we are, but we also are responsible to take care of our families. The key is to have everything in balance, with serving Christ at the top—even when it comes to our earthly jobs.

Our primary goal, Paul says, is to know Christ in every area of our life and as deeply as possible. We are to be consumed not with our work or our earthly status, but with Christ alone. When we place him first, everything else falls into place, making us better workers, better bosses, better fathers and mothers, and better people. The temporary gain (earthly attainments) becomes true gain as Christ permeates every area of our lives and transforms us in every way. But he must be first.

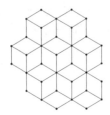

ADVANCING IN THE CHRISTIAN LIFE DESPITE WORLDLY FOES

(3:12–21)

In verses 7–11 Paul refutes the false teaching of the Judaizers by showing that all their legal works were not gains but rather must be considered loss to find the only true gain—knowing Christ. Here in verses 12–14 he corrects another theological error—the mistaken notion that one can be "faultless" (v. 6) or perfect in the Christian walk. Many Jews believed that a person could observe the Torah faithfully, make atonement for any transgressions, and be completely right with God—as the young ruler tells Jesus in Mark 10:20: "All these things I have kept since I was a boy." Perfection is impossible, but the goal of continual Christian growth in Christ is not only attainable but mandatory.

Paul calls his readers to adopt a mature mindset (Phil 3:15–16) and to follow his example (v. 17). These instructions were all the more critical in light of further false teachers who were living as "enemies" of Christ and endangering the church (vv. 18–19). Christian maturity, Paul says, demands that we live not for present pleasure but for future reward (vv. 20–21)—that we make the right choice between living for self or living for Christ, between focusing on earthly things (v. 19) or centering on heavenly things (v. 20). These vital choices will determine our eternal future.

PAUL ADDRESSES THE NEED TO PRESS
ON TOWARD THE GOAL (3:12-16)

The Key: Ongoing Spiritual Growth (3:12-14)

Taking stock and forging ahead (3:12)

In verses 4-6 Paul recounts all the "gains" he had attained in the past, going on to show the danger (in the present) of relying on those so-called achievements as grounds for having confidence in the flesh. Now he addresses an accompanying danger: We might assume that we have lived our lives so well to this point that we have reached moral and legal perfection, that we have "made it" in this world. There are two steps in correcting this serious error.

First, I must look at myself seriously and take an honest accounting of my life to date. This should tell me unequivocally that I have "not obtained all this or ... already arrived at my goal." If Paul was obliged to concede this of himself, how much more should we recognize this truth? The two verbs, "obtained" and "arrived," look back to verses 7-8 for their implied object—namely, knowing and gaining Christ.[1] Paul is saying that, ever since his conversion on the Damascus road, his goal had been to come to know Christ more deeply. Paul did not aim to become increasingly famous or to acquire greater power in the church; his sole focus was to gain more and more of Christ in every area of his life. The point here in verse 12 is that he had not reached this goal. He was still striving, still searching, still growing. As missionary Frank Laubach once said, "The closer I get to Christ, the further I realize I still have to go." The verb "already arrived" is literally "reached perfection" (*teteleiōmai*). It is possible that Paul's opponents were claiming they could keep the law so scrupulously that they could virtually bring heaven down to earth. Paul's point was

---

1. Others have seen the object variously as the righteousness of verse 9, the resurrection from the dead of verse 11, or the prize of verse 14, but the primary gain of verses 7-11 is definitely knowing Christ (vv. 8, 10).

that none of us will reach the ultimate goal until we stand before Christ. This is what we strive for, to be sure, but we can never truly attain it in this life. We will reach perfection in knowing Christ only "when the perfect comes" (1 Cor 13:10), when at Jesus' second coming we will be made "like him, for we shall see him as he is" (1 John 3:2).

The second step in correcting the error of perfectionism comes later in Philippians 3:12, where Paul identifies his singular aim as the day of Christ approaches: "I press on to take hold of that for which Christ Jesus took hold of me." The Greek verb translated "press on" (diōkō) refers to a vigorous, ongoing pursuit and may anticipate the athletic metaphor that comes in verses 13–14, portraying life as a race characterized by a strenuous effort to reach the finish line. That finish line is Christ, who had already taken hold of Paul on the Damascus road (Acts 9) and enrolled him in the race. In light of Christ and his great mercy, Paul longed to pursue Christ more deeply. The Greek phrase rendered as "for which" in the NIV might be translated better with the word "because" (as in Rom 5:12): Paul pursued Christ because Christ took hold of him. The picture is of Christ seizing Paul, taking him captive, and calling him to enter God's race. Paul in turn had thrown himself aggressively into that race, seeking to gain more and more of Christ.

The method for reaching the goal (3:13–14)

Forget the Past and Strive for the Future (3:13) —Verse 13 begins with the phrase "brothers and sisters," indicating to Paul's readers that he is admonishing them out of a heart of love. They were family, and he wanted them to experience the same spiritual growth he had. Expanding his point from verse 12, Paul tells how he is going to achieve his goal of grasping Christ more and more thoroughly. He begins by repeating the basic truth: He has not fully "taken hold of" his goal and continues to strive for it. This he states strongly and very personally. The Greek verb *logizomai* (NIV: "consider") returns to the accounting metaphor of verses 7-8; it means to look very closely (in this case at one-self) and to evaluate as accurately as possible the true state of affairs. Paul had closely calculated the columns of his life and drawn the correct conclusion: He wasn't there yet!

Paul outlines two stages for achieving his goal. The first is "forgetting what is behind." The image is powerful: Paul is like a runner refusing to be distracted by the competitors behind him. The effectiveness of this approach has been proven many times. I recall one of the most famous footraces ever, in 1954 between Roger Bannister of England and John Landy of Australia. Earlier that year, Bannister had become the first runner to cover one mile in less than four minutes; six weeks later, Landy beat Bannister's time by 1.4 seconds. Their first head-to-head matchup came later that summer and drew worldwide attention. Ninety yards from the finish line, Landy had the race won until he looked over his left shoulder to check for Bannister—who sprinted past him on the right to a dramatic victory. It became known as the "miracle mile."

The question in verse 13 is: What does Paul mean by "the things behind"? It is unlikely that this indicates his achievements *before* he had become a Christian (vv. 5-6), for he is speaking in verses 12-14 of the more recent past. More likely, "the things behind" refers to all that Paul had attained *since* becoming a Christian. It is important for us to note carefully what he is saying here—and what he is not saying. Paul does not mean that our service for Christ and the gospel does not matter; such a view would contradict the teaching about storing up treasure in heaven. Instead, he is insisting that we dare not sit back and be satisfied with our accomplishments. We can never have enough of Christ, and we should never become complacent about where we are in the Christian life and what we have done for Christ. We must be insatiable in our desire to attain more of Christ and to achieve more *for* him. By "forgetting" Paul does not mean to be uncaring; rather, he does not want to be distracted or led astray by dwelling on the past. We live for the future, not for the past.

Paul's second stage for achieving his goal involves "straining toward what is ahead." This continues the athletic imagery, depicting the runner with every muscle in her body taut and straining toward the finish line. This is what makes the Olympic Games so compelling; we are privileged to witness the world's greatest athletes at the apex of their careers, with their entire being and all their energy focused on winning. We have all seen runners collapse at the end of a race, lying on the ground and heaving for air while smiling from ear to ear at the sheer joy of reaching their goal. Victory is unbelievably difficult in any race, but it is worth the effort—and that is precisely Paul's point here. The Christian walk is not intended to be an easy stroll through life; it is incredibly hard work, demanding the utmost of our effort to live for Christ.

PRESS ON FOR THE PRIZE (3:14)—So far Paul has centered on the race itself, but now he identifies the finish line: "the goal to win the prize for which God has called me heavenward in Christ Jesus." For Paul, "the prize" means eternal reward; he uses the same analogy in 1 Corinthians 9:24, where he tells the believers to "run in such a way as to get the prize." The same image occurs in Hebrews 12:1-3, with the runners "fixing their eyes on Jesus," who is both the finish line and the prize.

In the Greek text of Philippians 3:14 the prize is defined as "the upward call of God in Christ Jesus." The meaning of this phrase is often debated among interpreters, who have proposed three main options:

1. The prize could be the upward call itself, meaning that Paul was focused on the privilege of participating in this call. However, this option does not fit well with Paul's own experience; his call had come on the Damascus road, and the race involved his current efforts to press on toward the

goal and win the prize. In other words, Paul's call was in the past, while verse 14 focuses on the present and future.

2. The prize could be heaven, where we dwell with Christ after winning the race. In ancient games the winner would be called up to a platform to receive the prize, which often was awarded by the emperor himself. So the picture is of God giving us the prize, a victorious life, as in 2 Timothy 4:8: "the crown of righteousness, which the Lord, the righteous Judge, will award to me on that day." This option presents the opposite problem—that of focusing solely on the future, while Paul was thinking also of the present race.

3. The prize could be a combination of the first two ideas. We are called to join and run the race, with the goal of knowing Christ more intimately every day. And we are called "upward" to a deeper and deeper experience of Christ, and the race will end with the final "heavenward" prize when we stand with Christ for all eternity. This is the best option; the prize is comprehensive, and the crown of life (Jas 1:12; Rev 2:10) and everlasting joy is Christ in all his fullness.

Overcome Differences with a Mature Mindset (3:15–16)

For the less mature: God will clear it up (3:15)

There is a strong play on words here as Paul addresses those who are "mature," using the Greek adjective *teleioi*. In verse 12 he uses a related verb to say (literally) "not that I already have obtained or have been perfected (*teteleiōmai*)." So in verse 15 he is saying, in effect, that "the mature realize they are not perfect." In other words, the truly mature will agree with everything Paul has said to this point and refuse to turn aside from the goal of coming to know Christ more deeply.

Paul's Judaizing opponents apparently were instructing Christians (Jews and Gentiles alike) to observe the Jewish law perfectly (see my comments on 3:12). Paul is saying that this was absolutely wrong, and that anyone with a mature knowledge of Christian truth would recognize this perfectionism as a false teaching. The Greek phrase translated "should take such a view of things" (NIV) reads literally "will think this"—reminiscent of 2:5, where Paul uses the same verb (*phroneō*) to say "have the same mindset." There Paul enjoined his readers to have the mind of Christ, while here his plea is that they would have the same mind as Paul himself. The guiding principle, as we will see in verse 17, is: "Follow my example, as I follow the example of Christ" (1 Cor 11:1). At the same time, Paul was aware of strong differences of opinion among his readers, so he goes on (in Phil 3:15) to address those who "think differently" about these matters. The phrase "on some point" most likely alludes to minor rather than major differences; since Paul does not specify the issues, it is difficult to know what he had in mind. Whatever they were, these minor points were keeping the Philippians from a mature understanding.

When such differences arise, Paul says, the church must make certain that it allows God to make the point clear. The Greek verb here is *apokalyptō* ("reveal," "uncover"), commonly used to indicate God's act of disclosing divine truths (Matt 16:17; Gal 1:16). Paul says nothing here about exactly *how* these truths will be made known. Discussion and debate among the believers are certainly part of the picture, as is the study of Scripture; behind it all, of course, is the leading of the Spirit. Paul's point was that every member of the congregation needed to open themselves up to God's deeper truths. And, as in first-century Philippi, the church today is called to adopt a mature mindset in Christ and remain open to the Spirit's guidance. Christians will always be discussing and debating points of doctrine, for we have all grown up with differing outlooks on what Scripture says. The teaching ministry of the church is an essential component of Christian faith that dare not be neglected.

For the mature: Live up to what you've attained (3:16)

Verse 16 reinforces the opening thought of verse 15: Mature believers should first of all take stock of where they are in their Christian walk (v. 15a) and then live appropriately in light of their relationship with Christ (v. 16). Note that Paul is not reprimanding the Philippians for failing to progress sufficiently, nor is he showing displeasure with their level of maturity. He accepted them as they were, called on them to appraise themselves realistically, and challenged them to move on from there and continue growing in Christ. The Philippians didn't have to reach a certain maturity level before the Spirit would guide them and Christ pour his strength into them. They did, however, need a desire to know Christ better and to yield to the Spirit more thoroughly. God wanted them to be faithful and committed, in accordance with the level of Christian maturity they had attained. Paul had taught them the gospel and its demands; now they had to make it the standard by which they lived and begin to grow in the depth by which they lived it.

This path of discipleship is not a passive approach—as though, after a season of preliminary growth, we can be satisfied with the level we have reached and just coast our way to heaven. Rather, Paul is challenging Christians to have an active, ongoing, and aggressive demand for more of Christ. We carefully take stock of our present status and level of maturity (v. 16), and then we put all of our effort into pressing on from there and progressing toward the goal and prize awaiting us (vv. 12–14).

PAUL ADDRESSES THE NEED TO LIVE NOT FOR THE EARTHLY BUT FOR THE HEAVENLY (3:17-21)

So far in this letter Paul has developed four paradigms or models of Christian behavior: Christ exemplifies humility (2:5-11); Timothy, love and compassion (2:19-24); Epaphroditus, perseverance in suffering (2:25-30); and Paul himself, steadfastness in the pursuit of Christ (3:4-14). He now calls on his readers to follow in their footsteps (v. 17), contrasting these Christian role models with certain false teachers who live for earthly things (vv. 18-19). Paul concludes the section by showing the importance of focusing on heavenly realities (vv. 20-21).

PAUL'S LIVING EXAMPLE (3:17)

Throughout chapter 3 (especially in vv. 4-14) Paul has used himself as a concrete example of the Christian who centers on future promises rather than on present earthly pursuits—someone who seeks to attain "the measure of the stature of the fullness of Christ" (Eph 4:13). In Philippians 3:17, he makes this paradigm explicit by urging the Philippians to "join together in following my example." The NIV translation somewhat loses the flavor of the Greek text, which reads literally: "imitators together of me be." The believers are to watch Paul as he imitates Christ and to do likewise.[2] As in verse 13 he expresses this challenge with loving concern, making it clear that he considered them "brothers and sisters." This was family advice!

Later in verse 17, the term "model" is the Greek *typos*, denoting a mark or mold that others can copy. A modern equivalent would be to look at a mature Christian life as a blueprint for others to follow in constructing their own lives. Furthermore, the Philippians were to "keep [their] eyes on" or "take note of" (Greek: *skopeō*) others like Paul. He was not the only model; those he had trained earlier (like Timothy and Epaphroditus) also could serve as mentors for the young Christians. In 1 Thessalonians 1:6-7 Paul shows another dimension of this pattern, describing how the Thessalonians had followed his example and become models

---

2. This is a matter not of self-pride but of good ministry sense. Everyone needs concrete examples to follow, and Paul is describing the basic method of Christian mentoring: "Follow my example, as I follow the example of Christ" (1 Cor 11:1).

for other believers. Three stages of modeling are reflected in these two passages—Christ to Paul, Paul to his churches, and the churches to other believers. This pattern is similar to 2 Timothy 2:2: "The things you have heard me say ... entrust to reliable people who will also be qualified to teach others." The Christian life is a relay race in which we pass the baton to the next generation of imitators/teachers.

THE INDICTMENT OF WORLDLY PLEASURE-SEEKERS (3:18–19)

Paul now turns to certain anti-models who should never be copied. In essence, in the same way the Philippians were to take note of examples worth following, they needed to be aware of people who posed a danger to Christ's community. There almost could have been two lists posted—models to imitate and those to reject. Some interpreters have proposed that these verses describe not a group of people, but rather a set of pernicious ideas that were prevalent in the first century; however, this view does not reflect the text here. Paul is discussing an actual group that was starting to gain influence, prompting him to say, "I have often told you before [about them] and now tell you again even with tears." Such language demands a concrete situation.

It is quite difficult—if not impossible—to determine the identity of these "enemies." The same questions we asked about the Judaizers in verse 2 apply here as well: Were they the same group as the opponents in 1:15–17 or the persecutors in 1:27–30? Were they believers or unbelievers? Now we add another question: Were they the Judaizers of 3:2? The language implies that they were part of the Christian community, since Paul uses the standard Greek term for denoting a Christian lifestyle—*peripateō* (meaning "walk" or "live"). Also, Paul "weeps" over them, suggesting they were insiders who had fallen away. Yet he also claims to have warned the Philippians frequently about these people, which points to a recurring threat from outside the church. The most likely scenario is that they were itinerant "Christian" false teachers who had begun to make inroads into the church at Philippi (similar to the Judaizers). However, Paul does not discuss what they were teaching; his emphasis is on their lifestyle, with all four descriptions in verse 19 relating to behavior rather than doctrine. For most of my teaching career I believed these "enemies" were the Judaizers, whose demands about Jewish dietary laws and circumcision ("mutilation of the flesh," v. 2) could explain Paul's assertions that "their god is their belly" and "they glory in their shame" (v. 19). However, in the course of reexamining the data to write this commentary, I recognized that verses 18–19 offer nothing that would make such a connection probable, so I have changed my mind. The language here seems to favor an earth-centered, libertine movement like that described in 1 John or Jude. These were "Christians" who preferred a pagan way of life, and Paul's tears stemmed from his deep concern both for these people and for those they were influencing in Philippi.

Their designation—enemies of the cross (3:18)

These people were likely frequent visitors of Christian communities in Macedonia, for Paul says "I have often told you before" about them. The description in these verses could fit the pagan lifestyle of all Romans, so these teachers may have been syncretistic, aligning Christian practice with pagan ideals and defending the Roman lifestyle as viable for believers. The dangerous current situation—that these false teachers had returned to Philippi and were making serious headway in influencing the Philippian church—is indicated in Paul's added comment "and now tell you again even with tears." The Philippian Christians had been taught many times about these pernicious ideas, yet they seemed to be yielding to them yet again.

The "walk" or lifestyle of these people, Paul warns them, proved that in reality they were "enemies of the cross of Christ." This is an extremely harsh indictment. The cross is the sole means of redemption and the reason for Jesus' incarnation (2:8), but it also is the sign of everything Christian. These false teachers apparently preached the cross, but the behavior they condoned and even encouraged put the lie to their preaching and made them "enemies of the cross." There is an important principle here. Right teaching that fails to produce right living is an abomination to God, who demands that belief be lived out in practice, that the mind influence the lifestyle. Those who claim to know Christ but fail to live accordingly are "enemies of the cross."

Four characteristics (3:19)

This is a frightening list, showcasing the terrible danger of trying to be at the same time a Christ-follower and a person of the world. As Jesus put it in Luke 16:13, "No one can serve two masters. Either you will hate the one and love the other, or you will be devoted to the one and despise the other. You cannot serve both God and money." Yet that is exactly what these false teachers were advocating and exactly what countless "Christians" today are attempting. Each of the first three descriptions centers on a contrast—destiny/destruction, god/belly, and glory/shame—while the fourth sums up the basic problem underlying the whole: the desire to inherit the heavenly while living for the earthly.

1. Their destiny is destruction—The "end" (*telos*) or destiny of a person refers to that which happens after their death: their eternal inheritance. These self-indulgent individuals were fated for eternal destruction (Paul was not referring simply to physical death, which is the destiny for every human being). Their anti-God behavior had made them enemies of the cross who were doomed to final judgment and the lake of fire. True believers have a heavenward call (v. 14) and are promised a bodily transformation (v. 21), but these quasi-Christians had no such destiny. They called themselves believers, but what awaited them was the fate of non-believers—eternal punishment.

2. **Their god is their stomach**—It is hard to know whether this is an allusion to the Jewish dietary laws or to their opposite, a libertine indulgence in the pleasures of the flesh. Several interpreters choose a middle path, suggesting a reference to the fleshly desires in general—a self-centered lifestyle. As stated above, the Jewish food laws don't fit the language, and some combination of the second and third suggestions is probably best. It is clear that Paul is not referring simply to their eating habits but is using a euphemism for their appetites in general, thus referring to a sensual lifestyle devoted to the things of this world. They worshiped the pleasure principle, which had become their god.

3. **Their glory is in their shame**—"Glory" is another term for boasting. Paul has spoken three times (1:26; 2:16; 3:3) about boasting in Christ, and now he describes its antithesis: boasting in self-indulgent pleasures, defined here as "their shame." First John 1:8, 10 confronts the faulty thinking of hedonists who claimed to be without sin despite their sensual lifestyle. They believed that their salvation was centered in their **gnosis**, or knowledge, meaning that they could live however they wished and their lifestyle would no longer be considered sin. Paul is addressing a similar situation in Philippians 3:18–19; these individuals pretended to be right with God, while their actions were completely shameful. Their life was filled with shame, and at the last judgment that shame would be manifested in their indictment from God, immersing them in shame.

4. **Their mind is set on earthly things**—Every aspect of their life is summed up in their earth-centered behavior. Their sensual appetites, shameful deeds, and final destiny were all dictated by their basic description as "earthly" from beginning to end. Every one of us must choose between an earthly and a heavenly pattern of thinking, and this

determines the actions that will result, as well as our destiny. The choice is between temporary pleasure and eternal joy, and this distinction is the basic message of this letter—indeed, of the entire New Testament. We all must choose between earthly pursuit and the heavenly prize, between fleshly gain and eternal reward.

The True Believers and Their Heavenly Destiny (3:20-21)

The answer to these false teachers and their earth-centered religion and lifestyle was the truth about heaven. This culminates chapter 3 and its emphasis on striving for more of Christ in light of the heavenly reality that awaits us. The point is that when we center on our future hope and the certain promise of eternal glory, the things of this world will fail to enslave us, and we will be enabled to live wholly for God.

Citizenship in heaven (3:20a)

The basic point is evident when we read verses 19b and 20a together: "Their mind is set on earthly things, but our citizenship is in heaven." The earth-heaven dichotomy is clear. Heaven is not merely a future reality we will someday enjoy; it is a present kingdom, and we have already received our citizenship there. From the moment we find Christ, we enter a new relationship with our homeland. We are no longer primarily American or British or German citizens. As the old song says, "This world is not our home. We're just a-passin' through." The reason why we imitate Paul and his team (v. 17) rather than the "worldly" preachers of verses 18-19 is that we belong to heaven, not to this world. In this world we are "aliens and strangers" (1 Pet 1:1, 17; 2:11), so why follow its ways?

Paul speaks extensively about this in Ephesians. We belong to "the heavenly realms," for since we joined God's family we have actually been seated with him in Christ (Eph 2:6-7), and as such we have spiritual blessings poured out on us as we dwell in "the heavenlies" (1:3). We have been made victors over the cosmic powers because the "whole armor of God" and his strength have been given to us (6:10–12), and we have proclaimed his wisdom to the evil forces of this world who are engaged in spiritual warfare in the heavenly realms (3:10). These assurances in Ephesians help explicate what it means to be a citizen of heaven.

The citizenship metaphor would have had special meaning to Paul and the Philippians. Unlike most Jews, Paul was a Roman citizen, probably a result of his family background and his upbringing in Tarsus. Roman citizenship gave him many advantages and rights (Acts 16:37; 22:25–28), just as he now affirms that Christians have special benefits as citizens of heaven. As for Philippi, it had been made a Roman colony and was considered a Roman city in another land (see the introduction to this commentary). In the same way that Philippi was to be a model of Rome in Macedonia, the church is to be a model of heaven in this world. There is a sense here of dual citizenship (in earth and heaven), but the latter has priority, demanding allegiance to a different set of laws and granting a greater set of privileges, spelled out in the rest of this section.

Eager expectation—the glorious body awaiting (3:20b–21)

Earlier in Philippians 3, Paul writes about "straining toward what is ahead," the heavenward prize (vv. 13–14). Now he spells out the nature of that prize, which will come to us via the One we await—"a Savior from there, the Lord Jesus Christ" (v. 20). Paul is looking ahead to the **parousia** of Christ, the core of all future expectation. Christ will come from heaven, where he has been since his ascension following his resurrection appearances. His return will unfold in events that Paul describes in 1 Thessalonians 4:13–18 (for the believer) and 5:1–10 (for the unbeliever; see also Rev 19:11–21). I believe these events will take place at the same time: Christ will come with the sound of the trumpet; those of us who have died will accompany him, and we will meet those believers who are still alive "in the clouds"; at that moment we will all receive our eternal resurrection bodies[3] and will join the angels of heaven and return to earth, where the battle of Armageddon will take place and the millennial reign of Christ will begin.[4]

The emphasis in Philippians 3:20 is similar to that of 1 Thessalonians 1:10: "to wait for his Son from heaven ... Jesus, who rescues us from the coming wrath." Jesus is both Savior and Lord, the One who will deliver us from wrath and bring this evil world to its end. The fleeting pleasures of this world are not worth sacrificing our eternal future. We have been redeemed from the slavery of sin and given over to God for an absolutely secure future. Why would we throw this away for temporary and ultimately unsatisfying things? Jesus as Lord Christ reflects that highest of all names given to him after his victory on the cross (Phil 2:9–11), and he is our Savior.

The reason why we should never even think of yielding to earthly pleasures is the subject of 3:21, which describes Christians receiving their resurrection bodies from Christ at his second coming. In that moment he will utilize "the power that enables him to bring everything under his control." As *Lord*, Jesus Christ is omnipotent, and as Almighty God he will exercise his power on our behalf—the same power through which he will destroy evil and exercise authority over his creation. This is the

---

3. The view espoused here is called the "post-tribulation" return, with the saints going through the Antichrist's reign. The pre-tribulational view believes that this will happen at the beginning of that period and that the coming down to earth will occur seven years later. The mid-tribulation view sees this as happening in the middle of the seven years, at the time the Antichrist comes to power.

4. This is the "premillenial" view, that after the Antichrist is defeated Christ will reign on earth for the equivalent of a thousand years (Rev 20:1–10). The amillennial position believes that this period is symbolic of the church age in which we now live.

moment described in 2:10 when "every knee will bow, in heaven and on earth and under the earth." Paul also writes about this to the Corinthians, explaining that Christ, after gaining complete control of his creation, will return that creation to his Father, "so that God may be all in all."

Part of that universal subjection of all creation, first to himself and then to the Father, will take place at the moment when Christ will "transform our lowly bodies so that they will be like his glorious body" (Phil 3:21). The verb "transform" indicates a total change of our physical bodies, but even that is a vast understatement! There has been no transformation like this in the history of creation. The phrase "lowly bodies" (NIV) reads literally "bodies of our humiliation" in the Greek text, which uses the same term that describes Christ humbling himself in 2:8. In verse 21 it connotes a lowly or weak mortal body, one subject to all the vagaries and ravages of life in this sinful world. At the age of 73 I can totally identify with this, having had heart surgery, my gallbladder removed, and chronic obstructive pulmonary disease (the result of lifelong asthma), as well as balance and walking issues. I look forward to my transformation more intensely than I can begin to say!

As a result of being transformed by Christ, our bodies will never again be lowly, for they "will be like his glorious body"—literally "conformed to the body of his glory" (Phil 3:21). In 1 Corinthians, Paul says that our body is "sown in dishonor ... raised in glory" (1 Cor 15:43), and he describes our new bodies as "heavenly" and "spiritual" (1 Cor 15:40, 44). As a result of this transformation, we will bear the image of Christ (1 Cor 15:49)—an assurance also given in 1 John: "When Christ appears, we shall be like him, for we shall see him as he is" (1 John 3:2). In this life we are conformed to Christ's death (Phil 3:10); in the next we will be conformed to his glorious, post-resurrection body. Paul says in Colossians that, when Christ appears, we "will appear with him in glory" (Col 3:4). We will share his glory for eternity. Thus we know that our transformation will involve a physical resurrection and an eternal body. There will be no more tears, death, mourning, crying, or pain (Rev 20:4), but only joy that never ends, as we bask in the presence of the Triune Godhead.

———

Earlier in chapter 3, (vv. 7–11), Paul shows the dangers of living in the past and allowing it to produce in us a sense of self-satisfaction. Now in this section (vv. 12–21) he centers on the importance of aggressively striving in the present to possess more and more of Christ. We must sufficiently "forget" our past accomplishments so we can focus on our present race and its goal of knowing Christ. We need to realize that we have not yet arrived at that goal; we dare not be satisfied with where we are, but rather must move on and continue growing in Christ.

The key to verses 17–21 is the contrast between the heavenly and the earthly: We are to be consumed by future heavenly promises, not earthly pleasures and attainments. Many worldly Christians and false teachers espouse a syncretistic Christianity that allows so-called believers to sample all the sensual delights of this world. It is clear in verses 18–19 that this will never work; as Jesus says in Matthew 7:23, "I will tell them plainly, 'I never knew you. Away from me, you evildoers.'" Only fools play games when their eternal destiny is at stake. Self-control is the only path to a satisfying life, for the destiny awaiting us is more than worth the sacrifice of worldly pleasures. We belong to heaven, and our future is an eternal, glorified body. Are temporary pleasures worth giving that up?

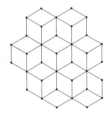

CLOSING EXHORTATIONS
(4:1–9)

At the close of most of his letters, Paul includes a series of final admonitions and a series of greetings; this is what we find in Philippians 4. The exhortations (vv. 1–9) are followed by a thank you for the Philippians' generous gift (vv. 10–19), a short greeting (vv. 21–22), and Paul's customary benediction (v. 23). The material here draws together many of the letter's themes and forms a natural consummation.

The command in 4:1 to "stand firm" especially has in mind the persecutors of 1:27 and the two sets of false teachers in 3:2 and in 3:18–19. Paul calls for a strong stance against these evil movements. The conflict between Euodia and Syntyche, mentioned in 4:2–3, may well have been the reason for Paul's focus on unity and selflessness in 2:1–18. The challenge to rejoice in 4:4 harks back to 1:18, and the admonition to be known for gentleness recapitulates the emphasis on humility in 2:3–4. The powerful section on the Christian mindset in 4:8–9 brings together all the passages about right thinking (1:7; 2:2, 5; 3:15, 19).

PAUL APPEALS FOR STEADFASTNESS
AND UNITY, (4:1-3)

STAND FIRM AGAINST FALSE TEACHERS, (4:1)

"Therefore" points back to chapter 3. The call to "stand firm" has in mind both sets of false teachers, from 3:2 and 3:18-19; Paul is commanding the Philippians to remain steadfast in light of these serious dangers to their relationship with God. Because fleshly (3:2) and earth-centered (3:19) religions opposed God's truth, and because the believers needed to strive for more of Christ (3:12-14) and focus on the future awaiting them (3:21), it was time for them to get serious about their Christian walk.

Many interpreters have called Philippians a "friendship letter." Paul feels deeply about these believers and wants them to know how much he cares. This loving friendship is reflected in 4:1, where he addresses the church using five affectionate phrases (we might call them "terms of endearment"), each of which is drawn from earlier in the letter.

1. "brothers and sisters" (also 1:12; 3:1, 13, 17)—Human siblings are related during this life, but Christians are united as an eternal, heavenly family. Everything Paul says stems from the reality that they, with him, belong to the family of God.

2. "you whom I love"—The Greek text here has the same adjective (*agapētos*) as in 2:12, where Paul shows the great affection he felt for these wonderful people by calling them "my beloved" (NIV: "my dear friends"). This idea is emphatic in 4:1, which uses *agapētos* twice (fourth word and last word); Paul is framing his thought here with a declaration that he loves the Philippians deeply.

3. "and long for"—This shows the extent of Paul's desire to be with them, which he also makes clear in 1:8: "God can testify how I long for all of you with the affection of Christ

Jesus." In 1:8, Paul uses a verb (*epipotheō*, meaning "desire greatly" or "strain after"); here in 4:1, he uses the related adjective (*epipothētos*, found only here in the New Testament). It's clear he was lonely for these beloved friends.

4. "my joy"—This is the main term Paul uses in the letter to express how he felt about the Philippians (1:4, 25; 2:2, 29). Paired with "crown," there is an **eschatological** nuance in which Paul anticipates the eternal joy they will share together in eternity.

5. "and crown"—This reflects the thought behind 2:16, where Paul talks about boasting in Philippians when they stand before the Lord together. This is the victor's crown, the prize (3:14) they will wear together after they win the race and receive their glorious bodies (3:21) at the end of the present age. The same idea is expressed in 1 Thessalonians 2:19, where Paul asks, "What is our hope, our joy, or the crown in which we will glory in the presence of our Lord Jesus when he comes?"

In light of all this, Paul calls on the believers to "stand firm in the Lord." In Philippians 1:27 he had challenged them to remain steadfast in light of persecution stemming from adversaries *outside* the church; here in 4:1 he urges them to remain steadfast in light of false ideas stemming from heretics *within* the church. In both cases the point was to remain grounded in Christ and entrenched in his gospel truth. The Philippians' anchor was sure and their future was completely secure. Thus the present difficulties and dangers had no power to move them from their God-given path. The means of standing firm are explained in chapter 3: Centering on their present and future upward call, they were to strive for more of Christ and less of this world. They are the children of God, citizens of heaven, and since they were grounded "in the Lord" they could not be moved. The idea here is similar to Paul's emboldening imagery in Ephesians: As soldiers wielding God's armor, the believers were to take their stand against the powers of evil, and when all was said and done they would remain standing firm (Eph 6:11, 13).

FIND UNITY IN THE MIDST OF CONFLICT (4:2-3)

Conflict between Euodia and Syntyche (4:2)

Paul sums up the issue of steadfast living in verse 1, and now he summarizes the issue of unity in the church. It is impossible to know how 4:2-3 relate to 2:1-18. These two women could have been instigators of a broad conflict in the church, with everyone else taking sides, or Paul could be mentioning them simply as an example of typical disagreements or personality conflicts. Either way, the fact that Paul addresses them by name shows their importance to the Philippian church. Clearly this was a conspicuous and divisive situation.

The names "Euodia" and "Syntyche" mean, respectively, "prosperity" and "lucky," and it is ironic that success and luck were at war with one another here. These were evidently two of the leading women in a church founded by a woman, Lydia, the patron of the church in Philippi (Acts 16:13-15). Paul repeats the verb "plead with" for each woman, showing that he is addressing them separately and refusing to take sides. He was concerned not with the question of who was in the right, but rather with the need for reconciliation and unity.

The instruction Paul gives here—"be of the same mind"—is identical to that of 2:2, suggesting that, one way or another, these women were at the root of the problem in Philippi. They must agree to disagree, so the church can find unity. While Paul is not saying they have to agree on everything, they must be like-minded on the essentials. This probably was not a doctrinal disagreement, but it was sufficient to cause conflict in the church. To be "in Christ" is to be united with him, and union with Christ means unity in the church. This unity obviously demands oneness in personal relationships. If the quarrel between these women was behind the earlier reference to "selfish ambition and vain conceit" (2:3), there could have been a battle for power and influence in the church. This is as close as we can come to a viable scenario. Evidently, these women cared more about themselves than about others or the church as a whole.

The need for the leaders to get involved (4:3)

As is so often the case in personal conflicts, the two women had been unable to reconcile on their own. They needed help. Yet in light of Paul's decision to intervene, their fellow church members apparently had been looking the other way, declining to get involved. There are important principles here for church life. Dissension rarely goes away without help, and the longer the people of the church refuse to get involved, the more dangerous the conflict becomes. This kind of situation, though it might seem innocuous, causes more church splits than any other. In this case, Paul had to step in and demand help from the congregation to end this dispute before it caused serious damage to the women involved and to the church.

Paul calls on his true "companion" or "yokefellow" to step in. It is a mystery why Paul does not name this person, especially since he does identify the women and refers later to Clement. For this reason, many interpreters have suggested that the Greek word for "companion," *syzyge*, might be a proper name; however, there is no evidence of this word having been used as a proper name in the ancient world. It is more likely that this person was so well known that Paul felt no need to name him or her. Nearly every prominent individual named elsewhere in Paul's letters has been suggested as this "companion": Timothy and Epaphroditus from chapter 2; Silas, who was Paul's companion on his journeys (Acts 15:40; 17:10; 18:5); and even Luke, who had been in Philippi when the church was founded (Acts 16:11). We cannot know. The important thing is that the church leaders at Philippi needed to get involved in order to bring reconciliation to these women and peace and unity to the church. The Greek verb translated here as "help" (*syllambanō*) connotes active participation; these women needed hands-on assistance in overcoming their differences. This is another critical principle for churches today.

The leadership role of these women is reflected in Paul's words "they have contended at my side in the cause of the gospel." The verb "contend" offers another athletic metaphor, implying the struggle involved in a contest. Euodia and Syntyche had struggled side by side with Paul in proclaiming the gospel in Macedonia, and they almost certainly would have been among the coworkers mentioned later in this verse.[1] It becomes especially serious when two such leaders lock horns, for each no doubt already had followers, and the conflict could have quickly escalated until it was raging out of control. So Paul asks not only his "true companion" but also his other Philippian coworkers—"Clement and the rest," who undoubtedly were close to Euodia and Syntyche—to step in and become personally involved as peacemakers. We do not know anything about Clement, except that this was not the author of 1 *Clement* (a letter from the church of Rome to the church at Corinth, written around AD 95—thirty-plus years after Paul wrote Philippians). "Clement" was a common Latin name, possibly indicating that its bearer was a Roman by birth. Clement might have been the leader of the Philippian church.

In an interesting aside, Paul observes that all their "names are in the book of life"—a frequent New Testament theme (see Rev 3:5; 13:8; 17:8; 20:12, 15; 21:27; also "names are written in heaven," Luke 10:20; Heb 12:23). This refers to the divine register of those who belong to heaven, an idea that stems from the lists of true citizens of ancient city-states (Pss 9:5; 87:6; Isa 4:3) and from the book containing the names of the righteous (Ps 69:28;

---

1. For women as leaders in the church, note Phoebe the deacon, Priscilla as coworker, and Junia as apostle in Romans 16:1, 3, 7.

Dan 12:1). The concept overlaps with Philippians 3:20, emphasizing that these leaders were citizens of heaven and secure in Christ as they awaited their final destiny. This is an apt image for the citizens of Philippi, who were proud of their Roman connection. In Christ they were citizens of a far greater kingdom—making the unity and peace of the church all the more critical.

PAUL CALLS THEM TO JOY AND PEACE (4:4–7)

THE NEED FOR CONSTANT REJOICING (4:4)

In this section, Paul churns out one command after another, each one restating a major theme of the letter. His first instruction here—"rejoice in the Lord"—is the most-repeated point in Philippians and in fact was the conclusion he had intended at 3:1 ("Finally, my brothers and sisters, rejoice in the Lord"). Paul felt real joy whenever he thought of these close friends who, more than any other church, had supported him and his ministry. Because of their partnership, it pained him greatly to learn of the hardships they were enduring—persecution (1:27–30), dissension (2:1–18; 4:2–3), and false teaching (3:2, 18–19). Still, Paul perceived the hand of God at work among these people and was confident of their commitment to Christ, so he could begin his closing admonitions with yet another call to joy: "Rejoice in the Lord always. I will say it again, 'Rejoice!'" All of Paul's other injunctions flow from this one, for joy makes each of the others possible. Every circumstance in life can be greeted with joy, but only "in the Lord," given that many situations are, in themselves, anything but joyous. Note the emphasis on rejoicing *always*. This reflects James 1:2: "Consider it pure joy ... whenever you face trials of many kinds." Paul rejoiced even when he was opposed by other preachers, so long as they were proclaiming the gospel (1:18). When that joy in the Philippian church was endangered by conflict, he could say, "Make my joy complete" (2:2). Even if he were to lose his life for the cause of Christ and for the Philippians, he would call on them to rejoice with him (2:17–18).

We must recognize once again that while Paul was penning these words he likely was chained to a Roman guard, awaiting word as to whether he would live or die. Another time he was in prison, in Philippi itself, he and Silas had been beaten severely and chained to a filthy wall, yet they had responded not with groans and curses but with hymns and praise songs (Acts 16:22-25). In any and every situation, the presence and involvement of the Triune Godhead calls for joy, because the Lord is in charge and is overseeing each circumstance to bring about good in the end (Rom 8:28). It is not our situation but the presence of God that determines the joy we feel. Like Paul, we are called to greet all the vicissitudes of life not with a weary sigh (though sometimes we just can't help it!) or an angry shout, but with songs of joy— for no matter the situation, we are "in the Lord," and all will be right in the end.

KNOWN FOR OUR GENTLENESS (4:5)

Gentleness couples with joy as the marks that set apart a Christian from the denizens of this world. Notice that our gentleness should be "evident to all"—non-Christians as well as Christians. When word gets out, Paul is implying, all those around us will be drawn to Christ. At my local church, I serve on a committee that focuses on congregational care. Ever since we made this ministry an emphasis ten or so years ago, we have become known as a caring church; every area of ministry has been affected positively by this ministry of caring for all in our congregation who are needy.

The Greek word translated as "gentleness" (*epieikēs*) is an interesting, multi-faceted term. In the context of how we treat others it means to be kind and gentle, while in relationships it is to be courteous and tolerant, and in legal situations it connotes leniency. When others make demands or mistreat an individual, the gentle person does not demand equity in return but willingly accepts the lesser portion and bears up under persecution, manifesting a longsuffering attitude and returning good to those who are doing evil. This injunction would have had profound meaning for the beleaguered Philippians, and it fits well the example of Christ in 1 Peter 2:23: "When they hurled insults at him, he did not retaliate; when he suffered, he made no threats. Instead, he entrusted himself to him who judges justly." A Christian who follows this model will invariably make a huge impact on those around him.

At first glance it seems strange that Paul adds the assuring note "the Lord is near." But given the strong eschatological cast of Philippians this makes good sense. Paul is asking these Christians to demonstrate their gentleness and goodness in an evil world, to become known for their steadfast resilience and loving nature, even to those who hated them. The truth of the Lord's imminent return is a reminder that God will right all wrongs, vindicate his persecuted people, and bring them to final victory. In other words, it will all be worth it, for he will turn our suffering to glory.

Frequently in the New Testament, a passage of admonition segues into a reminder that the end is coming soon (for example, Rom 13:12; 1 Cor 16:22; Heb 10:25, 37; Jas 5:8; 1 Pet 4:7). This is both a promise and a warning—a promise that our future glory will be worth our present hardship and a warning that God expects us to live in light of Christ's return and will hold us accountable for how we live. God's people are to be loving; as such, we do our part to rescue the perishing and usher in God's final kingdom.

PRAYER, THE ANTIDOTE FOR ANXIETY (4:6–7)

The means—prayer replacing worry (4:6)

These have always been two of my favorite verses. Paul begins with what I call the impossible command: "Stop worrying about anything." As soon as I say that I invariably start worrying anew, for it makes me think about everything that is going wrong in my life. With all the problems taking place in Philippi, the believers there were naturally anxious about their future. Paul's instruction to stop worrying reflects the sayings of Jesus in the Sermon on the Mount (see Matthew 6:25, where Jesus refers to flowers and birds as examples of God's care for his creation: "Do not worry about your life ..."). If God watches over his inanimate creation, Jesus says, how much more will he care for you (Matt 6:25–31)? Moreover, because the return of Christ is imminent (Phil 4:5b), we know that all of history is moving in our ultimate favor. As Paul expresses it in Romans 8:31, 33, "If God is for us, who can be against us? ... Who can bring a charge against those whom God has chosen?"[2]

Paul's answer to anxiety is profound: "In every situation, by prayer and petition, with thanksgiving, present your requests to God." This sums up the whole theology of prayer in a few powerful words.

1. EVERY SITUATION MUST BE COVERED BY PRAYER—The problem with trials is their infinite variety. We never seem to have the luxury of enduring them one at a time; they hit from every angle, often completely unexpected. The key to facing them is found in James 1:2–4 and 1 Peter 1:6–7: Every trial is intended by God to increase our faith and help us rely on him more completely ("the testing of your faith produces endurance," Jas 1:3). An active prayer life bathes every situation in God's empowering presence and enables us to "wait on the Lord" (Isa 40:31).

2. PRAYER MUST BE COMPREHENSIVE ("BY PRAYER AND PETITION")—Paul uses three different Greek words for "prayer" in this verse, not to distinguish separate kinds or aspects of prayer, but to stress its all-embracing nature. The Lord's Prayer (Matt 6:9–13) provides the model, including three necessary elements

---

2. Meaning any charge that matters in the long run. This was particularly ironic and powerful in Rome on the verge of Nero's pogrom against Christians!

of every prayer: worship (Phil 4:9), God-oriented petitions (4:10), and human-oriented petitions (4:11–13). True prayer does not begin with our needs; that would be self-centered. Rather, it begins the way any conversation should—with expressing our enjoyment in each other's presence. When we focus on a loving Father and care first about kingdom issues, our own difficulties filter down into their proper place, and we become aware that God and his Spirit are indeed more involved in our problems than we are. According to Romans 8:26–28, the Spirit is interceding for us more deeply than we are for ourselves! As in 1 Peter 5:7, you can "cast all your cares on him, for he cares for you."

3. WE ARE THANKFUL EVEN BEFORE WE PRAY—Thanksgiving permeates every aspect, both of our trial and of our prayer. Obviously this does not mean we are glad that these afflictions have come. Hebrews 12:11 says it well: "No discipline seems pleasant at the time, but painful." Our thanksgiving stems from God's vigilant watch over us. The presence of God the Father and of his Spirit makes the difference. This is a major theme in Acts, given all that the early church went through: Every crisis is an opportunity to watch the Spirit work! This is precisely where faith comes in. We are thankful that the Triune Godhead will take over, turning things around and giving us a way out (1 Cor 10:13). This doesn't mean our circumstances will always turn out the way we want; rather, they will turn out the way they *should*—for the best (Rom 8:28). We might die from an illness or be imprisoned like Paul, but God will bring ultimate victory out of every situation.

4. GOD IS THE FOCUS OF OUR PRAYER LIFE ("PRESENT YOUR REQUESTS TO GOD")—He is the true actor in the drama of life. It is he who is "made known" through our needs—not because he has been unaware of us, but because we need to actively bring our troubles to him. When we keep these anxieties to ourselves, they eat us alive; but when we pour them out to the Lord,

a sense of peace fills our hearts and minds (Phil 4:7). Our trials serve as a training ground, enabling us to use God's whole armor (Eph 6:10-12) and see his hand at work in our lives. And though it might be painful, we know that his discipline will "produce a harvest of righteousness and peace for those who have been trained by it" (Heb 12:11).

The result—the peace of God (4:7)

The result of an active prayer life is "the peace of God." We must remember that God variously gives three answers to our prayer requests. The one we hope for is "yes," but God is in charge, and in his wisdom and knowledge of what is best for us, he will at times say "no" (because what we are asking for is actually not in our best interests) or "wait" (because this is not the best time, but later on will prove just right). When we understand and acknowledge this threefold dynamic, prayer brings a deep peace to our hearts, because we know that our loving Father is involved and that whatever happens will prove best for us in the long run.

The peace of God parallels "the peace of Christ," which Paul insists in Colossians 3:15 must "rule in your hearts." Note the contrast here between human anxiety and God's peace. An earthly peace that is anchored in this sin-sick world will always be uncertain and subject to the vagaries of life. Paul is referring instead to the pervasive peace that characterizes God and comes to us as a divine gift. It is not just the opposite of anxiety, but the *solution*; God's peace is like the miracle cleanser that, when sprayed on dirt, just soaks it up and takes it away.

This peace, then, is not just an inner tranquility of soul; it is that and more. It is the Hebrew *shalom* that includes health, well-being, and prosperity. There is a sense of wholeness to it, a feeling that all is right with the world because God is in it. It begins with a personal relationship with God that extends to all the events that transpire in our lives. Our minds and hearts are filled with his presence, and in that way every trial takes on a different hue so that anxiety comes close to disappearing (though never totally, simply because we are human). This is why Paul says this kind of peace "transcends all understanding." This description has been understood in three ways: (1) This peace is beyond the ability of human reasoning to comprehend; (2) it is vastly superior to human perception and therefore heals the troubled heart more thoroughly; or (3) it is more effective and accomplishes far more than any human effort could ever attain. Paul's statement likely includes aspects of all three views, but the idea that this divine peace guards our hearts and minds favors the latter two. The emphasis is on the active working of God's peace in our lives, and the contrast lies between human effort and the activity of God in our hearts. He overpowers our minds and fills us with the Spirit's presence.

This peace, then, "will guard your hearts and minds in Christ Jesus." Paul does not use the regular Greek verb for "keep" or "guard" (*phylassō*), but instead chooses a military term (*phroureō*) envisioning a Roman garrison built around a town with a battalion of soldiers standing guard. This would have been a powerful image for Philippi, which as a Roman garrison town was the most secure city in Macedonia. Paul is saying that God's peace builds a fort around us, with his host of angels as guards to protect us from life's horrors. He is guarding us, ever vigilant, and we need fear nothing.

This does not mean that nothing bad will ever happen, but that those painful events can never truly defeat us. It is critical to remember this is in light of the promise in verse 5—"the Lord is near." All of us will pass through the valley of the shadow of death (Ps 23:4), but the point is we will *pass through* it. God will be with us every step of the way, and through it all we will be "more than conquerors" (Rom 8:37). Then, when life is over, we will be repaid for all that we have suffered and will inherit eternity. As Paul says all throughout these Prison Letters, this is accomplished "in Christ Jesus"—that is, in light of the fact that we are united with Christ and part of his body, the church.

PAUL DISCUSSES THE CHRISTIAN MINDSET (4:8–9)

RIGHT THINKING—EXCELLENT AND PRAISEWORTHY THINGS (4:8)

The Christian mindset has been another primary theme of the letter, centering on the need for like-mindedness (2:2; 3:15) and for the mindset of Christ (2:5). Paul culminates this motif with these verses. The point is that right thinking (4:8) will lead to right doing (v. 9). When joy (v. 4) and peace (v. 7) fill the heart and mind, both thinking and doing become heavenly operations.

In verse 8 Paul lists eight virtues of the proper mindset; the phrasing here is unusual, with the first six virtues introduced separately with "whatever" and the last two with "if there is any." Nearly all interpreters agree that it sounds as though Paul is quoting verbatim from a treatise on ethics, such as from a thinker like Aristotle or Seneca. This is evidently not the case, although the verse has all the earmarks of such writing; it seems to combine **Hellenistic** ethics with Jewish wisdom. It is difficult to discern any particular order, but if we attempt an organization the first four qualities would be inner virtues, while the fifth and sixth deal with external qualities (how others perceive us). These are all plurals, while the seventh and eighth qualities are collective singulars, functioning as summaries of what the virtues should be.

1. "whatever is true"—This is intentionally in the first position, and the other virtues flow out of it. "Truth" is meant comprehensively, beginning with Jesus as "the way and the truth and the life" (John 14:6; compare 2 Cor 11:10). All truth begins with the reality of God and centers on the gospel (Gal 2:5, 14). When we are characterized as true, we discern what is real from what is false and eschew hypocrisy. We are genuine followers of Christ.

2. "whatever is noble"—To be noble is to be filled with dignity and honor, as well as to be worthy of respect. The mind of Christ leads us to orient ourselves toward such people, as well as to *be* such people. The Greek word translated "noble" (*semnos*) is used often in Paul's Pastoral Letters to describe deacons (1 Tim 3:8), older men (Titus 2:2), and godly living (1 Tim 2:2). Paul is saying that our mind should be focused on majestic and honorable things.

3. "whatever is right"—The Greek word *dikaios* refers to justice and righteousness. Here it means fulfilling one's obligations to God to live justly—doing that which is right in his eyes. *Dikaios* language appears in many of Paul's foundational theological statements, such as Romans 1:17 ("For in the gospel the *righteousness* of God is revealed—a *righteousness* that is by faith") and 3:24 ("all are *justified* freely by his grace"). On the basis of Christ's redemptive work on the cross God declares us right (salvation) and makes us right (sanctification), and we respond by living rightly before him (the Christian walk).

4. "whatever is pure"—The Greek term Paul uses here, *hagnos*, belongs to a word group associated with being "in awe," "pure," or "holy"; in the Old Testament (**Septuagint**), it refers to people or things that had been rendered pure in a cultic sense. Later *hagnos* came to mean moral purity, and here it refers to a blameless life, untainted by the filth of the world. Paul expresses this idea often in his letters—for instance, the presentation of the saints to God as "a pure virgin" (2 Cor 11:2), the general need to "keep yourselves pure" rather than falling into sin (1 Tim 5:22), and the call for younger women to be "self-controlled and pure" (Titus 2:5). Here in Philippians, he is saying that a Christian's thought-life must remain centered on godly rather than earthly things.

5. "whatever is lovely"—This is a rare term in the New Testament describing that which is agreeable, pleasant, and attractive to all who see it. Paul says the mind should seek things that give pleasure and bring beauty into the lives of others. This is a wonderful quality, for those who possess it beautify the atmosphere around them; they are highly positive individuals who help the rest of us enjoy the lovely world God has given us.

6. "whatever is admirable"—The idea here is to be "spoken well of," worthy of admiration and praise. These are qualities, words, and actions that people find appealing and exemplary.

In the final two statements, Paul uses collective singular nouns to sum up the preceding six virtues and stress their comprehensive nature. He expresses these closing points as conditions of fact ("if" should be read to mean "since"), demonstrating just how "excellent" this list is.

7. "if anything is excellent"—Here Paul invokes one of the most important virtues in Hellenistic ethics, using a Greek term (*aretē*) encompassing all things considered good or excellent, whether human, animal, or even human-made (such as works of art and architecture). In the context of human virtues, this primarily points to moral excellence, which for Paul meant spiritual and ethical excellence in the sight of God.

8. "or praiseworthy"—This is the basic New Testament term for "praise," *epainos*, which usually refers in Scripture to the praise of God (both our praise of him and his praise of us). Here in this list of virtues, Paul likely means anything that leads to receiving praise from people around us. As a summary quality, it implies that we are to exemplify all the listed virtues, since they together enhance our place in society (on behalf of Christ) and draw praise from others.

In closing, Paul emphasizes that we are to "think about such things"—to carefully consider and reflect on these qualities, to allow them to permeate our minds and thereby guide our conduct (as we will see in the next verse). The present tense stresses the need to dwell continually on these virtues.

RIGHT DOING—WHAT THEY HAVE LEARNED FROM PAUL (4:9)

The virtuous qualities of verse 8 now must be put into practice. In Scripture all true thoughts are meant to be lived out in daily conduct; to remember or learn always means to act on that memory or learning. So here, the thought-life of verse 8 must necessarily lead to the life-deeds of verse 9. The central issue is not which qualities commend themselves and appeal to others, but rather which ones Paul himself had taught these Christians, reinforcing the importance of right thinking and right doing. He is saying that both in his teaching and in his actions he had exemplified these virtues and therefore could command the Philippians to apply them in their own lives.

Paul uses four verbs here, with the first two ("learned" and "received") referring to his teaching and the last ("seen") pointing to his exemplary life; the third verb ("heard") provides a transition, referring to both his teaching and his life. This statement sums up the earlier material on imitating Paul (3:4–14, and especially 3:17). He had brought the gospel to them, helped it take root in the church, and lived it in their midst.

What the Philippians "learned" refers explicitly to Paul's teaching; what they "received" involves him handing down the traditions he had received from the apostles and from the Lord himself, as well as in the creedal truths of the church—for example, the words of institution for the Lord's Supper (1 Cor 11:23) or the tradition regarding Christ's resurrection and post-resurrection appearances (see 1 Cor 15:3). The gospel teaching stressed the same virtues as did the Hellenistic world in which the Philippians had grown up, but now the presence of the Spirit added significant depth. In this letter Paul passed on to them the hymn/ tradition regarding Christ's incarnation (2:6–11) and shared with them his own personal history (3:4–14).

What the believers "saw" refers back to Paul's time in Philippi (Acts 16:11–40) and his model of suffering, dedication to the Lord, and love for the Philippian people. What they "heard" was not only his teaching but also other letters he had sent and the reports about his exploits they would have heard from time to time. Paul mentions these ideas earlier in the letter, referring to "the struggle you *saw* I had, and now *hear* that I still have" (1:30). In the midst of the persecution these believers were enduring (1:27–30), the privilege of witnessing Paul's example of perseverance and faithfulness to the Lord proved extremely valuable.

Because Paul embodied these virtues in the midst of extreme suffering, he had a right to instruct his churches to "put [them] into practice." This was true discipleship training—the readers learned about right living from Paul, observed him and the other mentors (3:17) living it out (3:17), and now they are challenged to exemplify it in their own lives. They were called to be Christlike, to pattern themselves after the concrete example of Paul, who continues to show them—even from prison!—what the Christ-ward path is all about.

In verse 7 Paul promises these believers "the peace of God," and now he assures them "the God of peace" will be with them. When we truly live for Christ and exemplify him in our lives, the God who brings peace and *is* peace becomes present with us through the Spirit (1:19, 27; 2:1; 3:3). Paul often uses this title ("God of peace") to describe the presence and power of God (Rom 15:33; 16:20; 2 Cor 13:11). God's peace stands guard over us (Phil 4:7), and the God who pours out his peace is present with us (4:9). Peace will reign among God's people when they are one with him and with one another. Peace and harmony are his will for his church.

———

Whenever we read this passage, we are deeply touched by its practical grandeur. Everything is present here to equip and enable every saint to live a worthwhile life in the presence of God and to make their Christian walk life-changing. The commands in these verses are both individual and corporate; Paul is primarily addressing church life, but he expects every member of the church to live out these qualities in their personal walk with Christ. The corporate cannot exist without the individual.

The first section of this passage (vv. 1-3) deals with two practical issues, the need to stand one's ground for Christ and the need for harmony in the church. The two intertwine, for a church cannot overcome inner conflict or outward pressure until it is grounded firmly in the Lord. Moreover, when it is anchored in Christ there will be little room for conflict, because every believer will be living a Christlike life (2:14-18).

The second section (vv. 4-9) contains equally critical principles for church life. We could almost call this a manual for church growth. The more I have pondered this passage the more I see an interrelationship among the points, which fall into three pairings. The first (vv. 4-5) challenges us to pursue joy and gentleness. With joy comes a kind, gentle approach toward others that fulfills the definition of humility in 2:3-4. The second pair (vv. 6-7) shows how life's anxieties can be dissolved with prayer, resulting in God's peace protecting us from the pressures and temptations of life. The third pair (vv. 8-9) invites us to carefully consider the virtues that equip us to be overcomers in life and then to act on them, allowing them to guide our conduct. Then the God of peace will take up residence in our lives and make us victors.

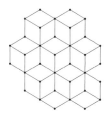

EPILOGUE: THANKSGIVING AND FINAL GREETINGS

(4:10–23)

Paul has already written about his gratitude and joy regarding the Philippians' friendship and all they had done for him (1:5, 7; 4:1), including their incredible gift in sending Epaphroditus to assist him (2:25-30). So in a sense the entire letter has been moving toward this passage, where he explicitly thanks them for their wonderful generosity. This is one of the major reasons Paul wrote this letter of friendship. In expressing his appreciation, Paul continues to be a model for us (as in 3:4-14), exemplifying effusive thanks for the contributions of others. The Philippians' great gift had touched him deeply, and his joy over their thoughtfulness permeates the passage.

Paul's words of thanksgiving lead straight into his customary final greetings, which are much shorter than in most of his letters (4:21-22), though filled with Christian warmth and centered on God's people as "the saints."

PAUL THANKS THEM FOR THEIR
GENEROUS GIFT (4:10-20)

THANKS FOR THE RENEWAL OF THEIR CONCERN (4:10-13)

Recognizing their concern (4:10)

With another note on the joy Paul felt because of these close friends in Philippi (see the commentary on 1:4, 18), he expresses his deep gratitude for the gift they had sent by way of Epaphroditus (2:25-30). Here Paul is describing his past rejoicing when he had first received the gift, but this joy obviously spilled over into the present whenever their gift came to mind—as it apparently did during the writing of this letter. The emphasis is on his *great* joy, leading to his lengthy and extravagant outpouring of thanksgiving over eleven verses. The expression of such joy always took place at crucial events, such as the birth of Jesus (Matt 2:10), the ascension (Luke 24:52), and the gospel's advance among Gentiles (Acts 13:52; 15:3). As Paul reflected on the extent to which these friends had partnered with him in the ministry of the gospel (1:4), showing such gracious concern for his needs, he was overcome with joy.

As we have seen throughout the Prison Letters (Ephesians, Colossians, Philemon, and this one), Paul's joy was always experienced "in the Lord." The Philippians' loving concern reminded him even more of the grace of Christ now coming to fruition through them, and it was in this context that he could experience true joy. So their earthly benevolence had been transformed into a heavenly gift. This is how Christian care takes place. God uses us as his tools to channel his loving care into the lives of others.

Paul tells the believers he is thrilled that "at last you renewed your concern for me." At first glance this could be seen as displeasure that their help had taken so long in coming, but he quickly dispels that false impression (see below). His language here is quite effusive; "renewed" conveys an agricultural metaphor describing springtime, when flowers and trees blossom forth with buds and shoots. So Paul is saying their gift had flowered forth, ending his drought with beauty and joy. The Greek word for "concern" (*phroneō*, used here for the ninth time in the letter; see also 1:7, 2:2) expresses the extreme "thoughtfulness" of the believers' gift. All in all, Paul was overwhelmed by the depth of their concern for him; their care had blossomed in his life and brought a new springtime of joy into his difficult situation in Rome.

He wanted to make sure the Philippians didn't take his remarks the wrong way, so he adds, "Indeed, you were concerned," again stressing the thoughtfulness of what they had done. He was fully aware that their loving concern had never flagged, even though for a time they had "had no opportunity to show it." We do not know why there had been no earlier opportunity, but the reason may have had to do with Paul's multiple imprisonments (Caesarea and then Rome—in total, four years and running) and perhaps also their own severe persecution (1:27-30) and the resultant "extreme poverty" of the Macedonian churches (2 Cor 8:1-2). Whatever the reason, the Philippians never stopped caring about Paul's situation, and he was overjoyed that they had taken this opportunity to give concrete proof of their concern.

That said, Paul's joy is centered on their wonderful friendship more than on the gift itself. The gift was anchored in their loving care, so his gratitude is grounded in their feelings for him, not in the tangible expression of that affection. Several interpreters have pointed out the commercial language Paul uses here. The Greek term for showing "concern" (*phroneō*) also means "have the same mindset," as in a business partnership (see 1:4, "partnership in the gospel"), so Paul is emphasizing the closeness of his ties with this loving church. They truly had become his partners in the gospel!

Contentment in every circumstance (4:11-12)

Paul wanted to assure the Philippians that his gratitude was not based on feeling deprived or having serious unmet needs. He had not been in dire straits, lacking basic necessities, nor was he still "in need" or desiring something more than he already had. We know from his letters to the church at Corinth that he had been criticized by some believers for living off their largesse (1 Cor 9:3-6; 2 Cor 12:13-14), and he was sensitive about such matters. He wanted to assure the Philippians that he was not asking for more or fixating on the size of the gift they had sent. He was neither dependent on nor beholden to them; his joy was in their loving concern and eagerness to partner with him.

Paul's aim was to ensure his supporters that he was happy and contented, regardless of his external circumstances. He expresses neither demands nor expectations, once again becoming a paradigm of the godly person, centered wholly on the Lord and relatively unmindful of his earthly situation. Still, he wanted his benefactors to know that this mindset had not come easily: "I have learned to be content whatever the circumstances." This was not a natural conclusion that had been obvious to Paul from the beginning of his ordeal. It had been necessary for him to "learn" it; it was a lesson from life, taught by the Lord the hard way. James expresses the same idea in different words: We are to "consider" or "count" our trials to be "pure joy," a perspective that develops over time as we are forced to rely on God and learn "that the testing of [our] faith produces perseverance"—which, over more time, teaches contentment. Paul did not reach this point this quickly or easily, but contentment was a necessary lesson that simplified his life and allowed him to depend much more on the Lord.

Contentment was an essential virtue in both **Stoic** and **Hellenistic** thought. It connoted self-sufficiency, being in control of oneself and one's emotions, using the power of reason to rise above adverse circumstances. Here in Philippians 4, Paul transforms this idea and infuses it with Christian content. His focus was sufficiency in God rather than self-sufficiency. The idea is to place ourselves under God's care (1 Pet 5:7) so fully that, whatever our financial or social situation, we depend entirely on him. Anxiety disappears, and God's peace takes over (Phil 4:6–7).

In verse 12 Paul spells out the meaning of "whatever the circumstances," stating, "I know what it is to be in need, and I know what it is to have plenty." Paul had definitely experienced both situations. The Greek text here contrasts being "humbled" or "brought low" with being "in abundance" or "prospering." Earlier in the letter, Paul says Christ "humbled himself" in his incarnation as a "slave," and God "highly exalted him and gave him the name above all names" (2:8–9). So in the circumstances described in 4:12, Paul was emulating Christ, the true model for us all. Paul's extremes certainly were not as sharp as those endured by Jesus, the God who became a slave, but he had known both good times and bad. He likely was raised in a wealthy home in Tarsus and had been sent to study with the leading rabbi of his day, Gamaliel (Acts 22:3). Still, he spent his apostolic ministry in relative poverty as a tent-maker and itinerant preacher (the major thrust in this context of the monetary gift). He also experienced extreme humiliation in the form of beatings, imprisonments, and deprivations (2 Cor 11:23–29). As a side note, I have found that the wealthy are often less content than the poor, perhaps because they feel they can never accumulate enough and are continuously comparing themselves with people who have even a little more.

To emphasize his point, Paul adds, "I have learned the secret of being content." The Greek verb translated here as "learned" (*myeō*) is known for its association with ancient mystery religions, referring to people being initiated into secret rites; it also was used as a metaphor for gaining insight (or insider knowledge) into an organization. Paul is saying that his "insider" experiences in the ways of God have led him to the amazing discovery that God is present in all events, whether they involve impoverishment or enrichment.

Contentment thus involves the sufficiency of God to turn all things around for the sake of the kingdom. What matters is not having everything go your way, but knowing Christ (Phil 3:8, 10). For Paul this had been proven yet again when, during a time of deep need, the Lord had led the Philippians to send their encouraging gift. To know Christ is to enter "the fellowship of his suffering" (3:10), and Paul had experienced time and again the benefit of that fellowship (Col 1:24).

He adds two further illustrations to reinforce his point: "whether well fed or hungry, whether living in plenty or in want." Paul's experiences of being "hungry" and "in want" are reflected in 1 Corinthians 4:11: "To this very hour we go hungry and thirsty, we are in rags, we are brutally treated, we are homeless." Here Paul is contrasting the apostles' circumstances with the opulence of the Corinthian church leaders; his point in Philippians is that, in Christ, he had risen above both extremes. He had experienced both, to be sure, but his earthly conditions had become irrelevant in light of knowing Christ, and he was Christ-sufficient either way.

Christ, the source of strength (4:13)

Many of us who grew up in the church can remember Philippians 4:13 as one of the memory verses that qualified us to attend summer camp. Yet memorizing isolated verses without considering the context often leads to misinterpretation, and this verse offers a good example. When we recite "I can do *all things* through Christ who strengthens me," we often regard anything we want to do as a real possibility—as though we become like Superman, able to leap tall buildings. Such an understanding leads to the error of triumphalism, thinking we can have or do anything we wish. This mistake becomes less likely when we consider the NIV, which rightly translates the verse: "I can do *all this* through him who gives me strength." "All this" (Greek: *panta*) refers back to "in any and every situation" (*ev panti kai en pasin*; v. 12) and therefore indicates the full range of our circumstances, whether characterized by need or abundance. Paul's point is that anything life threw at him could be handled through the spiritual strength he received in Christ. The Greek verb (*ischyō*) means "to have power or strength," so Paul is saying, "In Christ, I have the power to accomplish all this."

We must remember that Paul had suffered unimaginable hardships—not only arrests and years in jail, but also beatings, stonings, shipwrecks, and all manner of horrendous experiences (2 Cor 11:23-29). If anyone could speak definitively on coping with hard times, it was Paul. Yet he considered affluence a trial in its own right, for it tempted him to live for earthly possessions and luxuries rather than depending on Christ. As I mentioned earlier, the rich often seem more dissatisfied than the poor, for they never have enough material things. Paul handled both poverty and plenty in the same way, centering on Christ and his strength in every area of life. Because he surrendered every set of circumstances to the Lord, he could be content in any situation.

The key to it all is the final clause: "through him who gives me strength." Actually, the preposition commonly translated "through" is the Greek *en*, which means "in union with"—so the clause reads literally: "in union with the Empowering One." Throughout Paul's letters, "in Christ" expressions are a regular motif, and in Philippians this concept is the primary theme.[1] In chapter 1 alone we see the saints "in Christ" (v. 1), God's work in us continuing "until the day of Jesus Christ" (v. 6), "the affection of Christ Jesus" (v. 8), and "the fruit of righteousness that

---

1. Expressions using the Greek for "in Christ" or "in the Lord" are featured in Philippians 1:1, 13, 14, 26; 2:1, 24, 29; 3:1, 3, 9, 14; 4:1, 2, 4, 7, 10, 21.

comes through Jesus Christ" (v. 11)—and this is just the introductory section!

The Philippians' gift was a wonderful blessing that showed their deep affection for Paul, but he was acutely aware that it was Christ who had bestowed the gift, working through the Philippians. Ultimately, Paul was dependent on Christ, not his friends. Christ alone was empowering Paul to rise above his circumstances, giving him peace and contentment whether in times of hardship or abundance. This does not mean it is wrong for us to be thrilled with gifts and help from others; clearly, Paul was overwhelmed with joy at the Philippians' generous gift. But he saw the hand of Christ in it, as well. He was grateful for the loving support of his friends, but even more so for the power of Christ.

THANKS FOR THEIR PARTNERSHIP IN HIS MINISTRY (4:14–17)

Sharing in his difficulties (4:14)

Paul did not want the Philippians to take verses 10–13 to mean he was minimizing their gift, so in verse 14 he states, "It was good of you to share in my troubles." This may sound like faint praise, but it is not. In the previous section, he asks his friends to realize that his contentment in Christ did not imply a lack of appreciation for their support; he had not become a Stoic, detached from issues of need and untouched by acts of kindness. Now Paul returns to his earlier emphasis on the Philippians' partnership with him in the gospel (1:5, 7). Using a verb form of *koinōnia* (*synkoinōneō*; "to have fellowship with"), he refers to their walking through life together as full partners. They had shared with Paul many times via their concerns and prayers for him, and now they had shared with him concretely by sending Epaphroditus to assist him (2:25–30)— along with a monetary gift. Both the partnership and the gift were valuable in helping Paul overcome his "troubles" (or "afflictions"), a term used elsewhere in the New Testament to describe the hardships of life (Rom 5:3; 2 Cor 2:4; 7:4) as well as the sufferings of Christ (Col 1:24) and the tribulations of the last days at the end of the age (Matt 24:21, 29; Rev 7:14). Paul clearly had in mind his imprisonment and trial in Rome, along with the difficulties of spreading the gospel in the province of Macedonia.

None shared but the Philippians (4:15-16)

Intimacy flows throughout this section. To clarify the extent of his gratitude, Paul recapitulates the history of his partnership with this congregation, beginning with "as you Philippians know." Indeed, they knew as well as he did that their deep friendship went back to founding of the church at Philippi. He wanted to assure them that he remembered this precious early acquaintance as fondly as they did. This was a caring congregation that had labored alongside Paul from the very start. These believers had never forgotten his sacrifices to bring them to Christ, and he would never forget all they did in standing beside him during the hard times. In using the Latin form of the name "Philippians," he shows respect for them as residents of an official Roman colony.

Paul's reference to "the early days of your acquaintance with the gospel" is reminiscent of "your partnership in the gospel from the first day until now" (1:4), alluding to the church's inception during Paul's second missionary journey (Acts 16). Soon after planting the church at Philippi (and being miraculously freed from prison), Paul went on to Thessalonica. Although he was able to establish a church there, persecution forced him to leave and travel to Berea, a more receptive town ("more noble," Acts 17:11). However, agitators from Thessalonica followed him and sparked another persecution at Berea, prompting him to move on to Athens (17:13-15). In Philippians 4:15, the phrase "when I set out from Macedonia" likely relates to this turning point when Paul departed Berea and journeyed south to Achaia (southern Greece; the region of Athens and Corinth). During his time in Athens, Paul delivered his famous Aeropagus speech (Acts 17:22-31), but Acts does not record Paul founding a church in that city (though some interpreters think the converts of Acts 17:34 may have constituted a house-church).[2] After Athens, Paul continued south to Corinth—and from his two letters to that church we know all about the problems there.

Paul's point in Philippians 4:15–16 is that none of the other churches from that journey went on to share in his gospel ministry like the Philippians did. During his early weeks in Corinth, Paul had been obliged to support himself by tent-making (Acts 18:3), but after Silas and Timothy arrived from Macedonia, he "devoted himself exclusively to preaching" (18:5). Some interpreters believe Silas and Timothy had brought a monetary gift from Philippi that enabled Paul to stop making tents and work full time at evangelizing. In 2 Corinthians 11:8–9 he chides the believers at Corinth for their lack of support, saying, "I robbed other churches [ostensibly the Philippians] by receiving support from them so as to serve you. ... [T]he brothers who came from Macedonia supplied what I needed." In other words, the Corinthians' refusal to support Paul financially had forced him rely on contributions from other churches—money that could have been used elsewhere.

Paul describes the Philippian church as his partner "in the matter of giving and receiving" (Phil 4:15). These are technical terms used in commerce for financial arrangements—the settling of debts, buying and selling etc. Combined with the language of "sharing" and "partnership," this statement depicts Paul and the Philippians as partners in the business of selling the gospel to consumers, namely the pagan world. I admit this language may be startling, but it fits the imagery Paul is using to highlight this church's vital role in his missionary work. He portrays the financial support from Philippi as the means of distributing a life-saving commodity from heaven, the gospel.

---

2. There is no concrete evidence of a church in Athens in the first century; an established church at a later date is mentioned by Origen and Eusebius, but Athens remained pagan for centuries.

This arrangement is described as an exchange between friends and partners. The relationship between Paul and the church was cemented by the gift, yet they were drawn together by sharing not just the financial transaction but also the gospel itself. Only the Philippians had this kind of partnership with Paul, and that made them very special to him. The emphasis is on the reciprocity in their sharing: They had sent gifts and services (Epaphroditus) to Paul, and he had given them a share in his ministry of spreading the gospel—an enterprise in which they had participated with him. Each party had given the other friendship, affectionate care and support, and partnership in the work of the gospel.

Paul expands on this in verse 16, referring back to when he bid farewell to the Philippians and traveled on with his missionary team to Thessalonica (Acts 17:1–9). It is remarkable that the brand new church in Philippi supported him from the very start, particularly because these Christians, like others in Macedonia, were likely quite poor due to being ostracized by their pagan communities. Paul expresses this poignantly in 2 Corinthians 8:2: "In the midst of a very severe trial, their overflowing joy and their extreme poverty welled up in rich generosity." There is a side point implicit here: Paul did not enter any such partnership with the Thessalonian believers or any other church. Philippi was uniquely and spiritually enriched with the gift of helping, which in 1 Corinthians 12:28 refers to people whose caring hearts inspire them to aid the needy (compare Acts 9:36; Rom 16:1–2). Furthermore, as Paul continued his travels from Berea to Athens and on to Corinth, the Philippians kept sending their gifts "again and again" (NIV: "more than once"). They were an unusually generous church, with a heart as wide and deep as the ocean itself.

Paul's writing in this section brims with great joy; he clearly delighted in showing how deeply he appreciated these friends who shared in his work of spreading the gospel in the Roman world. Perhaps more than any other Scripture passage, these verses provide an incredible sermon on friendship and gratitude.

His desire—all this credited to their account (4:17)

Once again (see v. 11) Paul wards off any perception that he was interested only in the Philippians' money. We have no evidence that anyone in Philippi was making such an accusation; that scenario is unlikely, given the close relationship between Paul and the Philippians. However, as noted earlier, Paul had been criticized by some in Corinth (1 Cor 9:3–6; 2 Cor 12:13–14) and possibly in Thessalonica (1 Thess 2:9), so he was justly sensitive to any suspicion that he was trying to sponge off his congregations. Paul likely wants to make certain that no such criticism will be made in the future at Philippi. He thought of these friends too fondly to leave room for any doubts about his intentions. Rather than looking out for his own interests (2:4), he desires that "more be credited to [*their*] account." He again uses the language of commercial transactions to stress his unique partnership with this church. The Greek word translated "more" is *karpos*, the term for "fruit"; in a financial context, *karpos* referred to the "interest" that accrued from an investment. Paul wanted their profits from investing in him to continue to grow for their benefit.

This metaphor raises a significant question: When would the Philippians receive the benefits that were accumulating? Certainly Paul is referring to the **parousia** (the return of Christ), when God will repay all Christ's followers for what they have sacrificed for him and give them their eternal reward. But there is more than that—both an "already" and a "not yet." With a financial investment, interest accrues on a daily basis and is available at any time, though the full benefits will be paid in the future. So, following Paul's metaphor, God's blessing on the Philippians for all they had invested in Paul would be experienced every day as they took part in seeing the gospel bringing people into the kingdom, as well as in the unfolding of the longer-term effects of Paul's ministry. These present blessings were theirs at all times. Moreover, when Christ returned they would receive all the "fruit" they had earned, and as they used their gift of helping, their other spiritual gifts (the fruit of the Spirit, Gal 5:22–23) would increase exponentially as God blessed them in every part of their life (see v. 19, below).

THANKS FOR THEIR FRAGRANT OFFERING (4:18–20)

The abundance of their acceptable sacrifice (4:18)

As he wraps up his expression of thanksgiving and gratitude, Paul in effect gives the Philippians a receipt for their financial support. The verb *apechō*, another commerce term, means "receive full payment" and includes giving a receipt for that payment. Paul is saying, "You have paid in full, and here is a receipt for it." Paul is thrilled with their generous gift and wishes to go on record saying so.

To make certain they understand that he was not asking for more, he adds, "[I] have more than enough. I am amply supplied, now that I have received from Epaphroditus the gifts you sent." The contribution must have been sizeable, for Paul was still overflowing with gratitude a few months after Epaphroditus had arrived in Rome (2:25–30). Through these magnanimous friends, God had once again supplied Paul "immeasurably more than all [he could] ask or imagine" (Eph 3:20). The Philippians' generosity had brought Paul to a time of "plenty" (Phil 4:12).

At the end of verse 18, Paul switches from financial to sacrificial imagery, indicating a shift in focus from the contribution's blessing for himself to its acceptability to God. The Philippians' support was immensely helpful to Paul, but more importantly it had great value in terms of pleasing God. It was both a sign of the believers' friendship to Paul and a sacred offering to God. The horizontal, earthly deed had become a vertical, heaven-oriented worship event. To express the significance of the church's gifts, Paul gives three figurative descriptions:

- "They are a fragrant offering"—This builds on Paul's earlier portrayal of his possible execution as a "drink offering on the sacrifice and service coming from your faith" (2:17). The language of a "sweet-smelling savor" (KJV) depicts an animal sacrifice being burnt on an altar, giving off an aroma that was pleasing and acceptable to God (Lev 1:9, 13). In Ephesians 5:2 Paul calls the sacrifice of Christ a "fragrant offering," and here he uses the same metaphor to show that the Philippians' support was more than financial; it was sacred, bringing pleasure to the Lord as well as to Paul.

- "an acceptable sacrifice"—This phrase translates the first metaphor, pointing again to "the sacrifice and service coming from your faith" (Phil 2:17). The Philippians' gifts to Paul constituted a demonstration of faith, not just a monetary transaction. This was especially true in light of the church's poverty (2 Cor 8:2; see above on Phil 4:16). For these persecuted Christians, sending such a generous donation was truly an act of sacrificial giving.

- "pleasing to God"—God was even more pleased than Paul at the Philippians' selfless generosity. This third phrase enhances the sense of sacredness regarding their offering, both to Paul and to God. The idea of pleasing God is at the core of New Testament ethics, which Paul expresses well in Romans 12:1–2, describing believers' obedience as "a living sacrifice, holy and pleasing to God," and their transformation in Christ as proof that God's will is "good, pleasing, and perfect" (compare Eph 5:10: "find out what pleases the Lord").

The significance of this section is enormous. When we use our resources to uplift the unfortunate, we are giving a sacred love-offering to God, for these people we aid are his children, and what we do for them we are also doing for God. This is the central theme of biblical ethics: What we do to others (whether good or bad!) we actually are doing to God, and he will repay our compassionate deeds with divine blessing in our lives and eternal reward.

The reward—God meeting all their needs (4:19)

The Philippians' gifts constituted a sacred offering or sacrifice pleasing to the Lord, and Paul wanted these Christians to realize their present as well as future blessings (v. 17)—to know that "my God will meet all your needs." They had given sacrificially; now God would repay them handsomely. The reciprocity was not between the Philippians and Paul, but between the Philippians and the Lord. Paul's needs were "amply supplied" by their gift (v. 18), so now God would "supply" or "meet" their needs (v. 19; both verses use the same Greek verb, plēroō, meaning "to make full" or "to fill up"). The picture here—with the return on investment being paid by God—is similar to the one Paul paints in Ephesians 1:7-8: "the riches of God's grace ... lavished on us." Note the emphasis in Philippians 4:19 on "my God," which reflects a major difference between Christianity and pagan religions. The God of the Old and the New Testaments is a covenant God, a personal deity who loves and watches over his people. Paul's God was also the God of the Philippians, and all of them could bask in his loving care.

The phrase "all your needs" is, of course, as broad as possible, meaning every single need they had—social, spiritual, material, etc. Yet given the context of the passage (believers providing financial support; 4:11-12, 16, 18), uppermost in Paul's mind was God taking care of their material needs. Amid their poverty, the Philippians had sacrificed greatly to care for Paul, and now God was repaying them for their sacrifice by meeting all their needs. Still, we dare not exclude other areas of need, for throughout the letter Paul prays for the church's spiritual progress and social unity. Especially prominent would have been all the sources of anxiety in their lives (4:6), as well as their mindset (2:5; 4:8-9). Moreover, the prayer of 1:9-11 is closely connected with 4:18-20, and these passages form an **inclusio** that frames the entire letter. So "all your needs" includes each aspect of Paul's opening prayer— that the Philippians would abound in love and knowledge, discern what was spiritually best, and be filled with righteousness.

The source of God's supply is "the riches of his glory in Christ Jesus." This phrase contains three concepts, and each is important. First, the "riches" of God are mentioned throughout in the Paul's letters. This concept is especially prominent in the sister letters of Ephesians and Colossians: God lavishes his people with "the riches of [his] grace" and calls them to "the riches of his glorious inheritance" (Eph 1:7-8, 18); Paul preaches to the Gentiles the "boundless riches of Christ" (Eph 3:8); God makes known the "glorious riches of this mystery, which is Christ in you" (Col 1:27); Paul desires that people will have "the full riches of complete understanding" in order to know "Christ, in whom are hidden all the treasures of wisdom and knowledge" (Col 2:2-3). There can be no doubt that God is more than capable of meeting our every need—and, even more wonderfully, he is our loving Father who wants to do so.

Second, these riches pouring into our lives are "of his glory"— which means more than just "glorious riches." These riches are heavenly in origin and part of the glory of God, that transcendent splendor that is his alone; the God who dwells in unfathomable glory is sharing his riches with us. This supply goes beyond material or earthly provision, for he places at our disposal the resources of heaven itself. As we have noted before, there are "already" and "not yet" dimensions to this. Along with the fulfillment of our material needs, Paul was thinking particularly of the spiritual gifts we receive in the present, but the final payment will not be ours until we reach heaven at the end of the age (1:6; 3:21).

Third, this supply comes to us "in Christ Jesus," a key concept stressed in every part of the Prison Letters. Christ is the means by which God's riches come to us, as well as the sphere in which we experience them. It is through our union with Christ that all spiritual realities have come into our lives, and this refers both to his atoning sacrifice that has brought us salvation and to his abiding presence that we experience on a daily basis. God's riches are ours precisely in Christ. Paul and the Philippians were partners in Christ, and they participated in God's holy mission to the world in Christ—just as we do today.

Doxological closing (4:20)

The verse of praise does double duty, culminating both this section (4:10-20) and the letter as a whole. After meditating on God's riches and comprehensive supply for our every need, how could Paul not break out in praise? Such doxologies often close New Testament letters (for example, Rom 16:25-27; 1 Tim 6:16; 2 Tim 4:18; 1 Pet 5:11; 2 Pet 3:18; Jude 24-25) or major sections (such as Rom 11:36; Eph 3:20-21) by acknowledging the God who has made everything possible. All gifts come from him, and it is he who infuses life with meaning.

The doxology begins with "our God and Father." Paul's God (Phil 4:19) is the God of the Philippians as well, and he is Father of all. The letter's greeting was "from God our Father" (1:2), and the hymn to Christ in 2:6-11 ended with "to the glory of God the Father" (v. 11). In this there is likely an element of the *abba* (intimate Hebrew term for "father") theme, stressing God's deep love for and vigilance over his children. The whole letter has shown how intimately God cares for and watches over us.

To this heavenly Father, Paul ascribes the "glory" (Greek: *doxa*) or honor that he is due. However, *doxa* here does not mean simply to praise God; we do not "give him glory" as though he needs it from us. *Doxa* describes God's transcendent majesty, his **"Shekinah"** or glory dwelling in his creation. So we don't *give* him glory, but we *acknowledge* the glory that has always been his. We worship his eternal splendor. Glory is not synonymous with praise; rather, we praise God's glory.

The next aspect of this doxology is "for ever and ever," referring to the eternal aspect of God's glory—which is part of his nature, a divine attribute. The glory of God is not a created entity that came into being at creation or at the incarnation of Christ. It belongs both to the eternal past and the eternal future. To use the language we have been employing, it is the "already" and the "not yet." During the exodus from Egypt, the Shekinah glory was observed in the pillar of fire at night and in the cloud by day; this was the same cloud that filled the tabernacle and later enveloped the mountain at Jesus' transfiguration. The exalted Lord Jesus will return on the Shekinah clouds at his second coming, and we will live in God's glory for all eternity. It is indeed "forever and ever."

Paul closes the doxology with *amen*—the Greek transliteration of a Hebrew liturgical affirmation meaning "yes" or "may it be so." Each of the four sections of the psalms ends with a doxology that closes with "Amen" (Pss 41:13; 72:19; 89:52; 106:48), and this word also frequently concludes worship and doxologies in the New Testament (Rom 9:5; 11:36; Gal 1:5; Eph 3:21; 1 Tim 1:17; Rev 7:12). Here in Philippians, Paul intends for the reader to join him in worship and, as we do in churches today, affirm together God's eternal glory: "so be it."

PAUL GIVES FINAL GREETINGS (4:21-23)

REQUEST THAT THEY GREET EVERY SAINT (4:21A)

This closing is particularly intimate, demonstrating why many interpreters call Philippians a "friendship letter." In most of his letters Paul greets certain individuals by name, but here he asks that everyone in Philippi be greeted, reflecting how close he felt to these people. He doesn't want anyone to be left out. Elsewhere, he asks the people to greet each other (Rom 16:16; 1 Cor 16:20;

2 Cor 13:12), but only in Philippians 4:21 does he request that the believers greet "every saint" (Greek: *panta hagion*). Many translations of this phrase, such as "all the saints" or "all God's people," don't quite capture the comprehensive scope of Paul's instruction. Although the term *hagios* (see my comments on 1:1) is nearly always plural ("saints") in Paul's letters, here he specifies the singular form, clearly calling for "every single saint" in Philippi to be greeted for him. He felt deeply about every member of this church and wanted each of them to know the intensity of his affection. It is also possible that Paul deliberately skipped the opportunity to list people's names here due to the conflicts in the church, wanting to avoid any hint of favoritism. The churchwide greetings were to be delivered "in Christ Jesus," meaning that Christ was the source and sphere of their family relationship. All the Philippian believers were recipients of this letter, because they all belonged to Christ and were in union with Christ.

GREETING FROM COWORKERS AND SAINTS IN ROME (4:21B-22)

Paul also refrains from naming the coworkers who sent greetings to Philippi; instead, he identifies them generically as those "who were with me." This obviously meant his ministry team in Rome, coworkers like Timothy, Luke, Epaphras (Col 1:7), and/or Aristarchus (Col 4:10). Note that all of these parties—Paul, his associates, and the Philippian believers—were considered family, "brother and sisters" who loved each other in Christ. At the start of verse 22, Paul uses his typical expression "all the saints" (plural here, unlike the singular form in v. 21), referring to the Christians residing in Rome. He is not saying he has heard from each church member personally, but rather that the Philippian congregation was especially dear to the saints in Rome.

The reference to "Caesar's household" does not mean the immediate family members of the emperor (though some of them might have been included). Rather, the imperial household encompassed all the civil servants who ran the governmental apparatus of Rome, both freedmen and slaves. As a Roman colony, Philippi would have had connections to "Caesar's household," and this group likely included many of the people Paul names in Romans 16. Interestingly, Philippians is framed by references to government workers who had become believers, from Praetorian guards (1:13) to civil servants (4:22), showing Paul's successful ministry in Rome. Imagine—his capital trial, perhaps ending with his execution, had become one of history's great evangelistic campaigns!

CLOSING BENEDICTION (4:23)

This is Paul's standard closing, used in nearly all his letters. The "grace" (*charis*) of his opening greeting (1:2) is repeated at the end, making every detail of the letter a grace-gift from God. This is a Christian form of "farewell," the typical sign-off in ancient letters. There also is evidence that ancient worship services concluded with a benediction involving "grace."

The phrase "of our Lord" likely indicates the source of grace and is better translated "from our Lord Jesus Christ." This, too, parallels the start of the letter, where grace is said to come "from God our Father and the Lord Jesus Christ" (1:2); both expressions focus on the lordship of the exalted Christ as the source of the heavenly grace-gifts. Paul conveys something similar in 2 Corinthians, where he writes about his "thorn in the flesh." After he pleaded for God to alleviate his suffering, God responded, "My grace is sufficient for you, for my power is made perfect in weakness" (2 Cor 12:9). Through the Lord Jesus, human frailty is infused with grace and transformed into power.

In Philippians 4:23, Paul's prayer-wish is that this grace from Christ would "be with your spirit." It is interesting here that "your" is plural while "spirit" is singular. Some interpreters think this indicates the Holy Spirit, but that is doubtful. The emphasis is likely on the spirit of each and every one of us rather than on "the Spirit." Every one of the saints experiences divine grace from

God and Jesus, so no wonder his grace is sufficient! The stress on our "spirit" brings out the spiritual nature of Christ's presence with us; these are the spiritual blessings poured into us in Ephesians 1:3.

The benediction and the letter itself end with the second "Amen" of this section (with v. 20). Paul is adding his own "so be it," closing the letter with a prayerful "Yes!" to all that the Godhead was doing among the Philippians. God's grace was more than sufficient for the persecution they were suffering, the dissension and conflict they were battling, and the pernicious heresies the false teachers were spreading. In the midst of all these troubles, victory and joy were coming.

———

This closing section of the letter would make a terrific Bible study or sermon on friendship and gratitude, as it provides a wonderful example of an effective long-distance relationship. In Philippians 4:10–13, Paul focuses more on the believers' loving concern for him than on their gift. The message for us is significant: Relationships are more important than material benefits. Paul's sufficiency came from the Lord rather than from the accumulation of things. It was Christ's strength, not the amount given, that Paul relied on. Another lesson is about making our appreciation known. This passage is a powerful example of gratitude. Paul knew how to say thank you in such a way that the person being thanked understood the appreciation to be heartfelt.

Paul was especially thrilled that his friendship with the Philippians went back to the very beginning. Remembering the history of this relationship was a source of continuing joy for Paul (vv. 15–16), and we too in our periods of discouragement need to rehearse the love of close friends over time. Using business language, Paul brilliantly describes the depth of that friendship. The Philippians' gift to him constituted an investment that rendered them full partners in his gospel ministry, and they would receive the interest on their investment both in the present age and in eternity (v. 19). They had bought into God's business and become official partners with Paul. More than that, as colleagues in the gospel they were his friends. I often say to seminary students that if they serve in a church large enough to have a pastoral staff, they must become loving friends and not just colleagues. That is precisely what Paul and the Philippians had become.

Paul's final greeting is not just a throwaway section or a formality with no particular significance. It continues to demonstrate the love that existed at the core of this church and its relationships. Paul wanted to make sure every single person in Philippi knew how deeply he cared, and so he asks that "every single saint" be greeted on his behalf. Moreover, he had kept his coworkers and even the whole church in Rome informed about the Philippian brothers and sisters, and all were deeply concerned about their progress. Think of how encouraging it would be to know that one of the key churches in the world cared about *you*. This kind of support means more to missionaries than financial help. To know that churches are praying for them is a deep and abiding source of comfort.

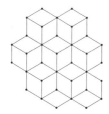

GLOSSARY

amanuensis: A scribe or secretary hired to write letters in the ancient world.

chiasm (n.), chiastic (adj.): Refers to a stylistic device used throughout Scripture that presents two sets of ideas in parallel to each other, with the order reversed in the second pair. Chiasms generally are used to emphasize the element or elements in the middle of the pattern.

christological (adj.), Christology (n.): Refers to the New Testament's presentation of the person and work of Christ, especially his identity as Messiah.

ecclesiological (adj.), ecclesiology (n.): Refers to the church (Greek: *ekklēsia*), especially in a theological sense.

eschatological (adj.), eschatology (n.): Refers to the last things or the end times. Within this broad category, biblical scholars and theologians have identified more specific concepts. For instance, "realized eschatology" emphasizes the present work of Christ in the world as he prepares for the end of history. In "inaugurated eschatology," the last days have already begun but have not yet been consummated at the return of Christ.

eschaton: Greek for "end" or "last," referring to the return of Christ and the end of history.

gnosis (n.), gnostic (adj.), Gnosticism (n.): Refers to special knowledge (Greek: *gnōsis*) as the basis of salvation. As a result of this heretical teaching, which developed in several forms in the early centuries AD, many gnostics held a negative view of the physical world.

Hellenism (n.), Hellenistic (adj.): Relates to the spread of Greek culture in the Mediterranean world after the conquests of Alexander the Great (356–323 BC).

inclusio: A framing device in which the same word or phrase occurs at the beginning and end of a section of text.

Judaizers: Label commonly used to identify a group of teachers who, in contradiction to Paul's gospel, encouraged Gentile Christians to observe the Jewish law and undergo the rite of circumcision. (The term "Judaizers" itself does not appear in the Bible.)

parousia: The event of Christ's second coming. The Greek word *parousia* means "arrival" or "presence."

Septuagint: An ancient Greek translation of the Old Testament that was used extensively in the early church.

Shekinah: A word derived from the Hebrew *shakan* ("to dwell"), used to describe God's personal presence taking the form of a cloud, often in the context of the tabernacle or temple (e.g., Exod 40:38; Num 9:15; 1 Kgs 8:10-11).

soteriological (adj.), soteriology (n.): Refers to the doctrine of salvation (Greek: *sōtēria*).

Stoic (n., adj.), Stoicism (n.): Relates to an ancient Greco-Roman philosophical movement that, during Paul's time, emphasized indifference toward one's circumstances as the path to personal freedom and peace.

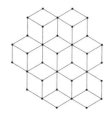

BIBLIOGRAPHY

Bockmuehl, Markus. *The Epistle to the Philippians*. Black's New Testament Commentary. London: A&C Black, 1997.

Bruce, F. F. *Philippians*. Understanding the Bible Commentary. Grand Rapids: Baker, 1989.

Cohick, Lynn H. *Philippians*. Story of God Bible Commentary. Grand Rapids: Zondervan, 2013.

Craddock, Fred B. *Philippians*. Interpretation. Atlanta: John Knox, 1985.

Fee, Gordon. *Philippians*. IVP New Testament Commentary. Downers Grove, IL: InterVarsity Press, 1999.

———. *Paul's Letter to the Philippians*. New International Commentary on the New Testament. Grand Rapids: Eerdmans, 1995.

Fowl, Stephen E. *Philippians*. Two Horizons New Testament Commentary. Grand Rapids: Eerdmans, 2005.

Hansen, G. Walter. *The Letter to the Philippians*. Pillar New Testament Commentary. Grand Rapids: Eerdmans, 2009.

Hawthorne, Gerald F. *Philippians*. Revised and expanded by Ralph P. Martin. Word Biblical Commentary 43. Nashville: Thomas Nelson, 2004. First published 1983 by Word, Inc.

Hendriksen, William. *Exposition of Philippians*. Baker New Testament Commentary 5. Grand Rapids: Baker, 1962.

Hooker, Morna D. *The Letter to the Philippians: Introduction, Commentary, and Reflections.* In *The New Interpreter's Bible,* edited by Leander E Keck, 11:467–549. Nashville: Abingdon Press, 2000.

Hughes, R. Kent. *Philippians: The Fellowship of the Gospel.* Preaching the Word. Wheaton, IL: Crossway, 2007.

Lightfoot, J. B. *St. Paul's Epistle to the Philippians.* 8th ed. Classic Commentaries on the Greek New Testament. London: Macmillan, 1913.

Martin, Ralph P. *Philippians: An Introduction and Commentary.* Tyndale New Testament Commentaries 11. Downers Grove, IL: InterVarsity Press, 1987.

Melick, Richard R., Jr. *Philippians, Colossians, Philemon.* New American Commentary 32. Nashville: Broadman & Holman, 1991.

Motyer, J. A. *The Message of Philippians: Jesus our Joy.* The Bible Speaks Today. Downers Grove, IL: IVP Academic, 1984.

Reumann, John H. P. *Philippians: A New Translation with Introduction and Commentary.* Anchor Yale Bible 33B. New Haven: Yale University Press, 2008.

Silva, Moisés. *Philippians.* 2nd ed. Baker Exegetical Commentary on the New Testament. Grand Rapids: Baker Academic, 2005.

Thielman, Frank. *Philippians.* NIV Application Commentary. Grand Rapids: Zondervan, 1995.

Witherington, Ben III. *Paul's Letter to the Philippians: A Socio-Rhetorical Commentary.* Grand Rapids: Eerdmans, 2011.

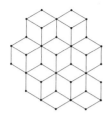

SUBJECT AND AUTHOR INDEX

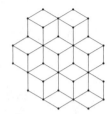

INDEX OF SCRIPTURE AND OTHER ANCIENT LITERATURE

Old Testament

Colossians

1 Thessalonians

Other Ancient Literature